SOUL SAUCE

by Ruth M. Bell

RoseDog❖Books
PITTSBURGH, PENNSYLVANIA 15222

All Rights Reserved
Copyright © 2004 Ruth M. Bell
No part of this book may be reproduced or transmitted
in any form or by any means, electronic or mechanical,
including photocopying, recording, or by any information
storage and retrieval system without permission in
writing from the author.

ISBN # 0-8059-9499-8
Printed in the United States of America

First Printing

For information or to order additional books, please write:
RoseDog Books
701 Smithfield St.
Pittsburgh, PA 15222
U.S.A.
1-800-834-1803
Or visit our web site and
on-line bookstore at www.rosedogbookstore.com

TABLE OF CONTENTS

ACKNOWLEDGEMENTS

COPYRIGHT

9 – 11 - 01 W. T. C.

It Made No Sense	2
Attack On America	3
What's Normal	3
Ground Zero	4
"Traffic?"	5
Wanna Help?	6
Six Month's Gone By!!!	7
They Are Gone!!!	7
Time To Stop Mourning	8
New York People To Boston	9
My Final 9-11 Thought!!!	10
A National Holiday	10
9-eleven by Devyn (Wray-Scriven)	11/12

Daily Inspirations

A Haitian Curse	14
A Hike vs a Gas Hike	15
A Lesson from the Straw	16
Appreciate your sweat	17
"Carnival/Parade"	18
Carol's Daughter	19
Chimps/Politicians	20
Conscience or Consequence	21
Dad	22
Do you have fun?	23
"Do you Remember?"	24
"Don't Go Back."	25
Going South	26
Grand parents week in Virginia Beach	27

Habit	28
Hate - Crime	29
Healthy lifestyle	30
Help	31
"Here We Go Again"	32
"How Do You Know"	33
"How Old Are You?"	34
"Huh?"	35
I'm Coming back—but not for long	36
In Bed	37
Japanese Asian Specialty	38
Justice for Sale	39
Keur N'Deye	40
Let them decide	41
Light	42
Love	43
Money for the Millennium	44
My paper-doll family	45
Remember	46
Speaking from the Grave	47
Juan Says	48
Street News	49
Teacher Shortage	50
The Daily Paper	51
The First Birthday	52
The Junk Drawer	53
Time	54
They're-r-r Back	55
Voting	56
Wonderful	57
You Just Got Here	58

My Life Story

My Beginning	60-61
Photos of my childhood	62-65
C.M.	66
Photo	67
Wishing	68
T.H.S.	69

Photos of the children	70-72
R.O.W.	73
Photos	74-75
V.H.	76
Photo	77
H.N.B.	78-79
Photos of my later years	80-83
Little Old Me [family pic]	84
No One To Talk To	85
Why!	86
My Virginia Journal	87-88
"My Will"	89

Family, Acquaintances and Friends

Barbara	91
Barbara and Tony	92
"Big Brother Wayne"	93
"Bill"	94
Leroy Comrie	95
Constella	96
Devyn	97
Eddie	98
Frankie	99
Hillary	100
"Kudos to Indio"	101
Liberty Mutual!!!	102
Mike Matarazzo	103
Monica	104
Ola	105
Otis	106
Ruth	107
Ken Sicari	108
Katherine Lee Tennyson	109
'Tre'	110
The McGhees	111
Seven-fourteen	112

Brooks Church

Dedicated to Winifred	115
"What a Pair"	116
Welcome	117
"THE MAN"	118
Faith	119
Rev. Joe—2000	120
The Answer	121

Adding the Sauce!!!

Are you too old?	123
Exercise	124
The male heart	125
Mental Block	126
Oversexed?	127
Once My Dream	128
Shacking	129
Tell Me	130
Woman's Day at the Vault	131

ACKNOWLEDGEMENTS

I must begin by giving thanks to my Lord and Savior Jesus Christ, without whom I would not be. I say I really do not know where this "gift" comes from but it is not from me..

To my daughters, Carole B. Sligh-Jackson and Rhonda Vanessa Wray for their Patience and feedback. To my granddaughter Devyn Wray-Scriven {aka Devynity} And Barbara Bethea aka {Afrikana Madonna} for inspiration and encouragement.

Thanks for everyone who supported me by purchasing my first book, "Changing Times." Thanks also to all the places that I have had the honor to perform:

Brooks Memorial United Methodist Church - Jamaica, N. Y.
Brooks Senior Center - Jamaica, N. Y.
Greater Framingham Community Church - Framingham, Mass.
Langston Hughes Library - Corona, N. Y.
Black Woman's Literary Guild - Roslindale, Mass.
Literary Circle of Friends - Virginia Beach, Va.
The "Vault" {Tone Bellizzi} - Jamaica, N. Y.
Channel 5 Good-Morning N. Y. with Jim Ryan

To those that have published my works:
Street News of N. Y. C.
The Press of Southeast Queens - Fresh Meadows, N. Y.
Fellowship Courier of Brooks Church.
New Millennium Poets - by Famous Poets Society

A special note of thanks to Ola Miles for being there for me.
Thanks also to the rest of my family, friends and neighbors who never Fail to keep me going.

9-11-01
W.T.C.

IT MADE NO SENSE.

How ironic that on this day
Our country's worst disaster came our way
Ironic because it's nine-eleven (9 - 11)
Waking - only thanking God in heaven.
I'll now remember today as nine-one-one (9-1-1)
The emergency call for everyone.
What a disaster - before my eyes
The World-Trade Center left the skies.
Anytime of day when I could see the towers
I'd sing "On a clear day" I can see for hours
I'd seen pictures of Oklahoma City and of war
But now our skyline's gone-never to be seen no more
Right now it's a disaster from here to Bangkok
It really hasn't hit us yet-we are still in shock
Unless he didn't come home-or you're missing one
It seems you're watching a picture that is being done
A picture being made to keep you in suspense
But when the shock wears off-you'll know this is no pretense.

WE HAD NO SELF-DEFENSE
A PICTURE MADE AT HUGE EXPENSE
A PICTURE WITH SCENES SO IMMENSE
YET STILL WE KNOW
"It Made No Sense"

Terrorism at the World-Trade Center
9-11-01.

"ATTACK ON AMERICA!!!"

I've looked at TV until I'm cross-eyed
Watching remains of people and buildings that have died
The wind - shifting - rains down charred pieces of dust
Because we are involved - praying becomes a must.
Ash falls everywhere - looking like snow
You watch it falling - the motion - it seems slow
F-16s buzzing over our head
Do I go out or stay home instead?
We are at war - can't see the enemy
Not like Dec. 7th - still a day of infamy.

9-11-01

WHAT'S NORMAL??

Getting back to normal - what does that mean?
Things are so chaotic - each days a different scene.
First "Ground Zero" - we're still not over that
Then the Anthrax scare - what's next on the format?
Now closer to home - I live near to JFK
A low plane goes down- what am I to say?
Terrorism, birds or even a bomb
Maintenance repairs just part of the norm
Guess we'll have to wait and see what's going on
But getting back to normal just maybe long gone.

"GROUND ZERO !"

Honoring the firemen, policemen they deserve it - it's true
All of them named "OUR MEN IN BLUE"-true blue
What about EMS, Con-Ed, Keyspan and Verizon too
They too lost some; yet they're still out there serving you.
How about the men that monitor the crane
Out there daily in the ruins, smoke, heat and rain.
The cook, cleaner, UPS, or mailman walking through the lobby
The tourist or visitor-there taking pictures cause it was a hobby.
How about the Red Cross, Salvation Army or a volunteer
Stand up and be counted "Let them all know we are here!!"
Doctors or nurses working around the clock
Even morticians working through bouts of shock.
Mayor Guiliani, commissioners and politicians in the daily paper
What, where or whom they saw - just a daily caper?
So if all your folks are home-others - you didn't know their name
Saying "I lost no one, knew no one" it is not the same.
We've all lost something, not a person, may be a service
Long lines, traffic jams - just because we're nervous.
So let's honor everyone - "Thank God you're alive."
To the terrorists say "We're Americans" we will ALL survive
We've all lost something be it big or small
Someday this will be over and only history will recall.
Children born in two-thousand - ten (2010)
Won't remember this how or when.
But those of us-here today will remember it till we die
We'll think of 9-11 always-with never a final good-bye.

9-28-01

"TRAFFIC ?"

We're worrying about trucks and vans that are coming in
If you're on a bridge; in a tunnel what difference where it's been
Not checking anything that is going out
Are we doing half of what this is all about?
Closing the barn-door after the horse was stolen yesterday
I know-so another one won't be stolen today-you say.
But if you're focusing on only one thing or place
Focusing on one nation, one country or on one race
Terrorists maybe trained and living anywhere
Let them know-we will overcome and together we all care.
So be it east coast, west coast or in between
Let them all know we're all closer-closer than we seem
Maybe this was meant for Americans to unite
For us all to become one - yellow, red, black or white.

9-27-01

WANNA HELP?

Can't go to "Ground Zero"-can't stand the smell or sight?
The rest of our problems-haven't disappeared-not even for a night
There's still work to be done-we've only just begun
How about big brothers/sisters taking kids out for fun?
People to visit the elderly-delivering "Meals on Wheels"
Delivering to those with AIDS who need wholesome meals
Adults and children who can't read or don't own a book
Old folks or young with no place to eat-no place to cook
Early riser? Serve coffee in any soup kitchen
Serving where they need you in Manhattan or in Brooklyn
Night owl? Staff a shelter, counsel a runaway; talk to one suicidal
Answer a phone 9-1-1 from one who's homicidal.
All these things must go on-you still can volunteer
Be it in the Bronx, Queens or Staten Island or even right here.

Inspired by Lenore Skenazy
Daily News 9-30-01

SIX MONTH'S GONE BY !!!

Today as I sat at the dining room table
I finally realized-6 months-I was finally able
To realize-it really happened-the shock is over
Feeling like awakening with a morning-after hangover.
Today for the first time I really shed a tear
Realizing so many have gone and I am still here.
To some-six months seems like yesterday
To others-it's just as if its happening today.
Now that I'm out of shock so are many others
Watch the health of people left behind-wives, children and mothers
With me-not losing anyone near-I could finally cry
With some despair can get so intense-could lead to suicide
Be prepared for their anger, mourning and sense of loss
But remember we are united-we all have to bear their cross.

3-11-02

THEY ARE GONE ! ! !

We'll never find closure for the one's that are missing
As we hug each other - whisper to each other while we're kissing
Good-bye - even though no body was found
They'd been cremated before the buildings hit the ground
Their soul was already gone - so we have to move on
So just realize - they're dead and they are really gone.

6-20-02

TIME TO STOP MOURNING.

I have sympathy for the families of nine-one-one
But it's time to go forward-mournings have been done
Some people mourn-wear black for many a year
They're mourning-but does that bring back those they held dear?
Some Irish even hire a professional mourner
Getting on with life-having a beer out on the corner.
The Jews are the best - do funerals right away
Doing it quickly-no waiting for another day
A week of mourning-food served by the spouse
Keeping busy-lots of people-if he was good or a louse
Yet they realize - it's time to get over it
Start going on - there's no time to cry and sit.
To children, spouses and parents left behind
Let's start to rebuild-starting with a monument or a shrine
Eventually this all will be history
Why we mourned so long - will be a mystery.

4-17-02

NEW YORK PEOPLE TO BOSTON.

I went to Boston to visit friends and family
Normally they'd have been coming down to see me
They said "After WTC we don't feel safe in the city."
Look what they'll be missing-Xmas activities-what a pity.
Missing Radio City, Macy's an a Broadway show-like you usually do
The Apollo, Rockefellers tree with lights red, white and blue.
Smell of hot dogs and chestnuts as they roast
A smell found no place else-along the whole east coast
I said; "The damage was started right there."
It wasn't ground level-it was done up in the air.
You had the terrorists living with you all the time
Planning and plotting how to do the crime.
So remember those planes from out of Boston came
So don't stop coming to N. Y.-that excuse is lame.
No matter what you think, say or do
Come to N. Y. and enjoy - for we don't blame all of you.
Think of this as a wake-up call-no time to snooze
With us becoming united-there'll be no more dynamic news.

12-02-01

MY FINAL 9-11 THOUGHT !!!

If I had my say for the World Trade today
I'd like to see them rebuilt - the way they were that day
As a memorial to the victims - divide there names for floors
Put a plaque with so many names by the elevator doors
Looking for a loved one - check in the vestibule
Which floor to go to - sunrise to sunset - that would be the rule.

9-01-02

A NATIONAL HOLIDAY ?

A year has passed no more time to mourn
It's time to build "Ground Zero" to be reborn
They talk about making it a National Holiday
They didn't do it for Dec. 7th -that's become just another day
Another day - yes in a year or two
A day to play golf or catch a sale or two
We're still in shock it's still brand new
In a couple of years-the states mourning will be just a few
So why start something that eventually will only mean
Something to those that lived through that disastrous scene.

9-11-02

It's like all I feel is desperation
When I think of a nation that's been robbed of thousands of lives
Not only was Bin-Laden's revolution live; it was televised
It gets me angry.
How many innocent by-standers were punished for a country's wrongdoing?
They said they ignored the warnings. They said they ignored the signs.
Once again the United States has under-estimated time.
Should I consider 9-eleven this country's retribution
For the centuries America's left it's people in ruin?
For the murder of thousands of natives to this land
For all the bales of cotton that were picked by black hands
For the Chinamen who built railroads then were told to go home
For Rodney King, Diallo, Dorismond; black men bought and sold
For Harriet's struggle as conductor of an underground railroad
I don't know.
But I pray America will cease its deceit
I pray America will not speak but just weep
I pray America has learned a lesson
I pray America will stop its oppression
I pray on my knees for relief
From this grief that I feel but there's none
Cuz' 9 one one took daughters and sons
Mothers and wives, husbands and fathers

So.....

With much sorrow
I pray that tomorrow
Will borrow more time for me to decide whether waving these American flags
Can take away the sad
And bring back the feeling of safety we had
I think no.
Bush seems to be torn to pieces
But U.S. tax money once funded Osama's legions
I see this interruption of our blatant complacence
Just erases faith from our faces
And anthrax leaves traces
Like the slaughter of our ancients
Find myself waiting to see 9-eleven's vagrants
Looking for oasis in the deserted pockets and empty wallets of their brethren
So 9-eleven is another number like 41 shots, 19 hits, 1492, and 1776
Each number marks the murder of another human-being; look how far we've come from
freedom
I walked home from Manhattan that day, just nervous.
How could someone commit this heinous crime on purpose?
I saw them crumble; I saw them collapse
Now they say it's okay to relax?

9-eleven
by Devyn Wray-Scriven

DAILY INSPIRATIONS

A HAITIAN CURSE

I believe in crossing a lot of people but Haitians are not one
Because they believe in their roots and herbs-they won't be outdone
Diallo (an African)they gave only a smile or a smirk
Paul Dorismond-one of theirs-time to get to work.

First came the health-slowly a deterioration
It only came to light with a routine examination
Then because of his brass and being so bold
He dissed his wife with no feeling-that was really cold
To flaunt his mistress to the media first
That's only the beginning of the Haitian curse.

Now comes his run for Senate-going down the drain
He says-"it's his health that has left him in a strain."
But messing with a Haitian- ask anyone
His troubles - be it health, marital or political-it's just begun.

Remember a lot of people don't believe in this
This is only one person's feeling but I've seen it work
They've evidently dismissed him with a fatal kiss
Eventually all will fall in line - just like real clock-work.

5-24-00

A HIKE vs. a GAS HIKE

This is the time of the year I usually start to walk
Cherishing sights, sounds, and listening to others talk
Shoulders back, arms pumping, head held high
Breathing in and out, seeing grass and blue sky.

This year more than ever it means more
I'll have to walk further as the gas prices soar
Walking will save me money and reduce the stress
Prevent strokes, add years to my life make my weight less.

If I buy half as much gas and walk twice as far
It will be better for me and better for my car
Me for my health and less weight to bear
Even my car and wallet will have less wear and tear.

3-15-00

A LESSON FROM THE STRAW

The majority of New Yorkers, Yankee fans or not
Wonder why a wealthy, talented man knowing what he's got
Has a self-destructive affair with a little drug
Facing his wife, his team with a face that's smug.
Drugs are used to self-medicate emotions or pain
To hide internal distress - denials are all we gain
Emotional turmoil that holds you in its traps
However inevitably leads you into a state of relapse.

Addiction is a life-long relapsing disorder with no cure
It's not really a personal weakness and doesn't care if you're rich or poor
While relapse is predictable — it shouldn't be condoned without
                              Consequence
Short-term rehabs is not enough time it just deters another recurrence.
You have to get at the bottom to find the reason for the stress
But it has to be on their terms they seek counseling not because we press
Strong external demands are sometimes needed to counter the
                              Powerful need
Getting them into treatment is fine - be it for alcohol or weed.

For them to choose a life of recovery - they must recognize their
                              Self-abuse
It takes hard work, impulse control and no more giving a lame excuse
They have to take responsibility and not compromise
To mentally itemize what's going on and not feel victimize.
To commit ourselves to a drug-free society
We have to help them all towards sobriety
If they have talent, fame or wealth
Be homeless or poor - just let them know it's for their own health.

Inspired by Peter Provet
Op-ed page
Daily News 3-10-00   3-12-00

APPRECIATE YOUR SWEAT.

You. heard the saying "don't sweat the small stuff."
But if you don't sweat-on your body it can be rough
On romantic nights sweat can be really good
Walking down the aisle-sweating could cause an attitude.

This time of the year-the sopping season
There's good and bad sides of sweating all with a reason
An adult can lose I to 3 pints in cool weather
In hot weather up to 5 gallons-making you light as a feather.

We don't see it-it cools by evaporation-a good side
When it doesn't evaporate-it doesn't cool-a bad side
We'd have to pant like a dog to really survive
In the absence of sweating we could not stay alive.

Drs. Say "Sweat is a little salt, potassium and mostly water."
To replace what you lose-you must replace the water
Eight cups a day is standard for an adult
If you sweat a lot, drink more for the best result.

Cool water and rubbing alcohol can hold back sweat for a couple hours
While the alcohol you drink, more you sweat as you devour
So alcohol and tobacco causes increases in you adrenaline
Put them together besides sweating it effects your encephaline.*

Some American tribes believe sweat is good for physical healing
Modern day spas use sweats to cleanse the skin-and that's appealing
So to sweat has it's good side and bad
But if you don't remember you'll wish you had.

*(chemical in the brain)

8-20-00

"CARNIVAL/PARADE"

it's time for the West Indian carnival and parade
where everyone is preparing for the masquerade
it's an imagery of a melting pot
where the main song playing is "Hot, hot, hot."
Bajans, Grenadians, Jamaicans from all the Indies
An the mixture of them and their native goodies
A potpourri of aromas that fill a three mile stretch
Islands represented by the food they fetch.
From Jamaica-curried goat and peas and rice
Don't forget ackee with an exotic spice
From Trinidad-roti and aloo pie
Even plantain-some they boil-some they fry
And don't forget conch salad from the Bahamas
Or men dressed in Kente' cloth-looking like pajamas
Come witness, the culture, music or the food
Whatever you're after-you'll get in the mood
It will be an experience for you to remember
You'll still be thinking about it even in December.

COME!

9-1-00

CAROL'S DAUGHTER

Have you ever heard of "Carol's Daughter" in Fort Green
She caters to the Nubian African-American queen
With more than 75 products for our black body and hair
White folks oils and salves can't even quite compare.

Lisa Price is the owner and she's Carol's daughter
She makes you feel and smell good - starting from the water
Yes! Our skin gets dry and even gets real ashy
She has the products to make us feel good - yet very classy.

With the mellow jazz and the welcoming ambience
To come in - see the mural and furniture's a homey experience
The customers range from expectant mothers
For labor massage oil - to dreadlocked brothers
For Loc Butter for scalp-nourishment
For a young black woman - what an accomplishment.

There are the "jellies," lemon-grass cleansers for the face
Especially concocted and made for the black race
Honey Pudding salve or cocoa-scented salts for bath
Try them, buy them, take them home for the aftermath.

1-16-00

CHIMPS/POLITICIANS?

Chimps and politicians know all about flattery
They both use their wiles,-some sweet-some buttery
They know its manipulate but it works
They give a smile and pull your chains-with a jerk.
Flattery knows no bounds especially in an election year
Both candidates manipulating us across the country far or near
In democracies we the people hold the election with our power
So they butter us up until the last voting hour.
We know its flattery yet we fall for it
It hits the target-which is our vanity-be it bit by bit
Even male chimps kiss the foot of the alpha male
Hoping he'll share his food or his main female.
Male chimps also play with the children-bio or orphan
Like our candidates kissing kids before a tasteless luncheon.
Its old as the pyramids-that were built to flatter King Tut
Troubadours serenading women with a song-be you a queen or a slut
During the Renaissance with flattery and merit
Without lineage-if you had these two it was a credit.
In America flattery found its richest soil
You could go from a clerk - to a boss with a little toil
So today smooth-talking candidates can still distract us
With disturbing truths, a smile and agendas to discuss.
So this fall separate the message of plain bull
Don't let them pull over our eyes the proverbial wool
So to let them know you've been aware
You're listening to things-showing that they care
Get out and vote by your head and not heart
And remember flattery on the menu was only a' la carte.

8-30-00

CONSCIENCE OR CONSEQUENCE

How many times have you heard
Let your conscience be your guide
If you believe and live by God's word
His word will guide you as He stands by your side.

When we face matters of conscience
We too can do the right thing
If we face the world with a vengeance
Leave the consequences to God of whom we sing.

Gov't. officials maybe tempted to accept a bribe
Employees asked to arrange numbers or a false report file
Students face temptation - like cheating of plagiarism
Families face situations from leniency to rigorism.

All of this is only conscience testers
Helping us to see if we're serious with integrity
We know the real test comes when we decide what to do
That the consequences become a necessity.

The greatest protection against the wrong decision
Is trusting in God if we decide to do right
That we have a job or school to go to because of our precisian*
Leave the consequences to God and it will be all right.

*(strict observer of rules.)

1-15-00

"DAD"

What's an admirable quality common in a marmaset, siamang, sea horse or jacana?
There's a squirrel-size monkey, ape, and not one a horse and a robin-sized wading bird
But the male of each of these take care of the young-is the mama and the papa
If only our Christian fathers could nurture, warn, teach or counsel by their word.
They too could be one to take on the task of a father-by modeling the Christian life-and his children teach
Be you biological, step, god or grandfather-like in Ephesians 6:4 rear them by training-not by preach
Christ like example is father's greatest gift to a child-seasoned with wisdom and compassion
Be it your own child, step, god, or grand-child-teach them how to love with a passion.
Some of us had fathers that were physically present but emotionally absent
While others have fathers that are neither here or never been there
You may have an alcoholic father-where the climate of fear is real resentment
You may have to change your feelings to show you really care.
All children have to drop this feeling toward their abusive or absent dad
So it won't be passed on to the next generation
To be uplifted with our family and never be sad
To become a new race with no medal of decoration.
Think what could happen if we emptied our hearts of bitterness
Make peaceful relationships our goal
Forgive our ancestors for abuses with tenderness
A start in making our lives completely whole.
If our dad has failed us-rely on God's grace
Let's strive to be the kind of dad-we've never had
It won't be easy but our heavenly Father's place
Is to help us become a very good dad.

8-24-00

DO YOU HAVE FUN?

Take a look at children it's easy for them to have fun
Every things a potential joy even if it's just a run
Between obligations and responsibilities as we grow older
We give up fun and pleasure to be an old householder.

We say "work is not to be fun - fun is for the child."
We want to let loose but afraid to get a little wild.
Sometimes you feel guilty or selfish if you indulge in fun
For a high quality of life it's necessary - for everyone.

What you consider fun may change at different stages of your life
A good book, conversation or even dinner with your wife
It could be an event, dancing, singing, or even playing cards
Playing with the children, grandchildren or pets in the backyards.

Maybe its arts and crafts, the movies or volunteer work
Combing flea markets, visiting model homes may even be your perk
If its puzzles, games, joining a club or taking a class
Make a point to do something every day for fun - so life will not go pass.

2-12-00

"do you remember?"

DO YOU REMEMBER WHEN YOU WENT INTO A HARDWARE STORE
YOU'D BUY NAILS, BOLTS, NUTS AND SCREWS AND VERY LITTLE MORE?
LATER WALLPAPER, PAINT, OIL LAMPS MAYBE A POT OR PAN
MEN SITTING AROUND A POT-BELLIED STOVE AND PLAYING COON-CAN?

HOW ABOUT A SPECIALTY SHOP WITH BARRELS OF RICE, FLOUR OR
 CORNMEAL
COFFEE SOLD BY THE BEAN TO BE GROUND-THE SMELL JUST
 WALKING IN-WAS IDEAL
IN THE DRUGSTORE ONLY A PHARMACIST AND AN ICE-CREAM JERK
BANANA SPLITS, SUNDAES, MALTS TO EAT BY YOURSELF WAS A
 LOTTA WORK

WHEN YOU WENT TO SHOP-NO ASSOCIATED, KEY FOOD,OR PATHMARK
 WHERE YOU BUY EVERYTHING FROM FOOD TO SOCKS
ONLY HAD ROYAL-SCARLETT, GRISTEDES (FOR THE RICH)OR THE A. & P.
 TO BUY FOOD FRESH OR CANNED ONES IN STOCK
YOU WENT TO THE BUTCHER FOR YOUR MEATS
TO THE BAKERY FOR BREAD AND SWEET TREATS.

WE ONLY HAD 5 & 10 CENT STORES LIKE KRESGE OR WOOLWORTH
NO K MART, WAL-MART WHERE YOU BUY ANYTHING ON EARTH.
YOU WENT TO A GAS STATION ONLY FOR GAS OR OIL
THEY MADE SURE YOU DIDN'T DRIVE AWAY WITH A WINDOW THAT
 WAS SOIL.
THEY PUMPED YOUR GAS, CHECKED YOUR OIL AND IT WAS ALL FREE
NOW YOU BUY CANDY, CHIPS, CIGARETTES OR EVEN A CUP OF TEA.

YOU SAY YOU DO REMEMBER?
WELL! YOU'RE OLDER THAN YOU TOLD ME -
YOU WERE REALLY BORN IN MAY AND NOT IN DECEMBER.

10-12-00

"don't go back."

EVER TOLD YOUR CHILDREN SOMETHING YOU'VE BEEN TOLD?
SOMETHING THAT'S BEEN DRILLED IN YOU FROM THE DAYS OF OLD?
AND YOU KEEP ON IT-EVEN TELL YOUR GRANDCHILDREN TOO
A MESSAGE YOU HOPE THEY'LL LISTEN TO AND FOLLOW THROUGH.

MY GRANDMA SAID "TWO THINGS NEVER GO BACK TO
A JOB OR A BOYFRIEND (NOW THEY CALL IT "MY BOO")
BECAUSE THE REASON YOU LEFT-IN THE VERY FIRST PLACE
WILL EVENTUALLY ESCALATE AS YOU AGAIN MEET FACE TO FACE.

I BELIEVE THERE'S NO GOING BACK TO SOMETHING THAT
YOU'VE LEFT
THEY THINK YOU NEED THEM
-YOU THINK THEY MISS YOU-
TO EACH OTHER YOU ARE DEAF
SO ONE THING REMEMBER-IT'S OVER-FORGET THE PAST
IF YOU GO BACK-YOU'LL BE UNHAPPY CAUSE IT WILL NEVER LAST.

9-7-00

GOING SOUTH

I've finally visited the south at the age of seventy-eight
I'm glad I got to see it - before it was too –late
I kept looking for the people - working in the field
Picking cotton, peanuts or tobacco - it was not all real.
The south I had envisioned is not what I saw
An the southern hospitality was a whole lot more
The people I met - treated me as part of the family
Hearing children saying — "Yes maam, yes sir" was a real reality.
I was looking forward to hominy grits and catfish
I got that and other foods-not knowing-asked "what's this dish?"
I expected to see little houses - like run-down shacks
Only for blacks - by the river or the railroad tracks.
But I've been in so many places - from the outside it looked small.
Inside there's almost three apartments divided by a hall.
I stood upon a hill and as far as I could see
Land owned, farmed or lived on by the family called McGhee
It's just living in the north - only further apart
Houses not so close but more love from the heart
If I ever get a chance to go back- another year or day
I may even be enticed to remain longer or even stay.

7-7-00

Grand parents Week in Virginia Beach.

Have you ever decided your grands needed to have some fun?
So you call for the kids of your daughter or your son
You ask for a week - praying they'll let them come
Seven sets of grandparents – plan-leaving nothing to random.

Pool parties with pizza, hamburgers and franks
Day before they come you all run to the banks
For money for extra activities, food and clothes they forgot
Hoping they don't get homesick before your patience's shot.

You pray to God for the weather - with no rain
You've planned for the movie and the museum-which become your gain
You even enjoy the museum in the Portsmouth city
The Disney picture "The Kid" a movie with love and pity.

With all of you working together - the time went fast
God was good with the weather - but it's over at last
Will I be looking forward to this next year?
Don't look for an answer now - my thoughts are not clear.

I must remember - I can't correct in one week what they've done
Or what they've got away with in the other fifty-one
By next year I'll forget my frustration, extra cooking, washing and ironing
                                That was done
And then my reply to you will be "Oh! Well I'll try it for another one."

I'm writing this - I'm only the great grand-ma
To all you grandparents-you all deserve a star
As for me-next year I'll stay home
Wait until it's over before I come.

8-14-00

HABIT

I tell my friends, at home and in the church-"I'm free at last."
But I've been in such a rut - I still live in the past
First I'd never been able to tithe - had to save for food
Now that I can depend on me-I can and do-it feels good.
I bought cheap toothpaste or used baking soda and salt
When I reach for it now - I tell myself it's time to halt
I know I can afford better when I go out to shop
But I still buy mediocre - can't reach the top.
When I look at prices - I still let out a groan
Still use a three minute timer for my telephone.
It's really true - habits bad or good are hard to break
So I'm going to learn to treat myself better - starting with a steak.

5-26-00

HATE - CRIME

Hate - crime has really become gruesome
When you combine gay and black into a twosome
Hate - because he was black or hate because he was gay
To be either - I believe you were born that way — had no say.

Both racial and homophobic hatred go hand in hand
Why can't N. Y. adopt a hate-crime bill in our part of the land?
Forty-one other states have - are we so behind?
Can't we send a message - we know what's going on we're not blind.

If gay or lesbian - it's common to be rejected by the family
Since 1 out of 10 will grow up to be either - must we harm them bodily?
Educate the people that homosexuality has always been in existence
And hate is an equal sickness that needs our assistance.

We have to provide a secure environment for the young
When they have no where to turn let us be the one
To address their concerns and offer them aide
Where they can come have a good time and not be afraid.

Where being young gay, or black is not a crime
Where hate is an unknown evil and we have the time
To provide a safe and nurturing place.
Come to think of it - let it be for any race.

3-30-00

HEALTHY LIFESTYLE

In youth you take for granted rewards of good health
As you get older - freedom of pain is worth more than the wealth
It starts from watching your weight - habits that are quite harmful
Quit smoking, trade ginger-ale for gin and don't eat until you're full.

Drink the water, incorporate nutrition and get the exercise
Start to lose so you won't be called the one that's oversize
You can lower cholesterol and pressure if you have ideal weight
Reduce joint problems, heart disease and diabetes won't be your fate.

Good nutrition is better than the calorie count
And don't forget to put exercise into your account
You'd be surprised what stress does in your every day life
It can affect you more than any kind of physical strife.

Stress can be acute or chronic - make your pressure rise
Cause infertility, a stroke or a heart attack in disguise
Try to take deep breaths as you walk each day
Fifteen minutes of sunshine when you're on your way.

Cut back on the cigarettes and upon the drink
Go to bed early, get plenty of sleep and you'll soon be in the pink.

2-11-00.

HELP

Some words to shock our nation
Is- "What's being done on black education?"
The saying "My mother didn't raise no fool"
But she did if she didn't insist on you going to school.

With no education - be you black or white
You are wrapped in blackness-can't see the light
If you can not read or can not write
Everything you get is all a hard fight.

Teach us history with both sides in view
Educate us all so we can earn our due
Let us relax and realize that we all had a part
In the building of our country-from days of horse and cart.

7-8-00

"here we go again"

Last year I wrote a poem about Amadou Diallo and 41 bullets
This year its Patrick Dorismond who with 1 bullet his blood coagulates
On a side walk he dies because he said "No"
He rejected a drug deal and a persistent cop - SO

Here we go again - Rudy's narc division
Make at least 5 arrests with no revision
He says "there's no quota - but 5 collars a day are expected from each team"
To be persistent, so you don't blow your cover is part of the scheme.

If you cross Rudy he brings out your records - when at six you stole a pack of gum
At 13 - something never went to court but its still on record but nothing
                stating how far You've come
Even when a man bought up the fact of a red-light trap
They found a 13 year traffic ticket and he was arrested in a snap.

The Diallo shooting was an accident so it was said
Another year, another unarmed man - Rudy talks with his mouth and not his head
If it was an accident - it was the part of a miserable plan
Then harsh words spoken - as they stepped over another innocent dead man.

                    3-19-00

"HOW DO YOU KNOW"

when I was coming up - drugs - mama made from herbs
from things she grew, found wild or growing by the curbs
she usually boiled it and made it into a tea
nasty tasting stuff but it cured what ailed me.
Now Mom's of today wonder - is my kid using a drug
Me (being a grandma) don't know what to look for as they give me a hug
They say it's a combination of things to really look for
How they withdraw from family functions when you see them at the door
If they come with friends are they the new or old
They all look and dress alike as they come cross your threshold
Is their attention span short - they don't listen like before
Music playing, TV blasting - always with three or more
They say the eating or sleeping habits get erratic
They're either in the dumps or everything's ecstatic
They say look out for deterioration of appearance and hygiene
But there's no dilated pupils, bloodshot eyes - even fingernails are clean
As far as attitude changes - always had a mood swing
Cry as if their heart was breaking - 5 minutes later break out and sing
No dishonesty or stealing from any family member
Always told white lies - as far back as I can remember
So if they have a problem - I'd be the last to know
I feel sorry for parents looking for a show as they grow.

11-20-00

"HOW OLD ARE YOU?"

how old are you? How long have you been here?

Do you remember when movies were only 12 cents?
A movie, frank, and root beer - 25 cents was your expense
You took back bottles for 2 cents and ran errands all week
So you could see a cartoon, movie and a serial (to which you'd shriek)
Left on a cliff hanger - so you'd return next week.
Now to go to the movies you almost need a mortgage
And that doesn't include popcorn, soda or a sausage.

How about you smokers - for "WINGS" - ten cents a pack
Most of you bought tobacco in a little beige sack
You rolled your own with no addition
It was for mostly men - that was a tradition.
Women that did it was called loose or a slut
To keep a reputation they did it behind doors that were shut
Now to smoke a cigarette it's almost $5.00 a pack
To get the kick you add to it - be it smack or crack
You can't go to the movies and sneak a smoke
Even though it costs more - your enjoyment is a joke

As for me - I've never smoked - can't afford a movie
I pop my own popcorn and tell myself - this is groovy.

HOW ABOUT YOU?

12-13-00

"HUH?"

after sight the next is hearing loss
this one makes the family least tolerant and cross
people outside the family are so understanding
the family with strangers - their manners are outstanding.

Your spouse screams "You're driving me crazy
You don't want to hear me - because you're lazy."
One daughter makes fun of you - the other says "Oh! Never mind."
The oldest son gives you a dirty look saying "He's worse than being blind."

The youngest son -just like his mom- he will just yell
Under his breath says "fuhgeddaboudit" or go to hell
They ignore you when you're having dinner - just as well eat alone
They say "You listen better when you're talking on the phone."

You love talking to the grands - they don't seem to mind
That you. can't hear too well - and getting a little blind
You don't get a dirty look when you ask them to repeat
So when they're here you sit with them when it's time to eat.

1-20-00

I'm Coming Back - but not for long.

I came to Virginia Beach last summer to spend a couple of weeks
Had such a good time - even enhanced my poetry techniques
I met the New Virginians and even went to book-club meetings
Bar-b-ques, pool parties and weight - watchers teachings.
Now I'll be back to all of you people I missed
But what made me stay so long was for peace of mind and bliss
Now that I have that at home - can't stay too long
Won't wear out my welcome - have to go where I belong.
I'll always keep in touch with my extended family
I might be there spiritually and not really bodily
But my heart is with you all as I'll go home real fast
For my home is now a home - not like a prison - in the past.

5-6-00

"IN BED"

Have you ever laid in bed and heard the sorrowful sound of a foghorn?
The lonely blow of a locomotive passing through?
In the dark all alone feeling so forlorn
You experience this every night - it's nothing new.
It makes you feel so lonely - everything going away
As you twist and turn - hoping and waiting for the day
Now again it's all silent - all's faded away in the dark
You finally fall asleep - hearing only a lone dogs bark.

9-27-00

"JAPANESE ASIAN SPECIALTY"

have you heard of Kans Yoshida of JAS mart?
You can go shopping there and you'll really need a cart.
It's a Japanese convenience store on the West Side
Where the store is packed with people and they sell with pride.

There's all sorts of ingredients needed to cook Japanese dishes
Fruit drinks, blended coffees and frozen foods for your wishes
It has everything from Wasabi (a pungent root) to Q-tips
Ice cream, Japanese magazines and Wasabi chips.

Pocky sticks (with flavored coating)the selection is extensive
For tofu, miso soup and seaweed for sushi-nothing is expensive
Quite popular with the students is the sushi box for lunch
Shiseido cosmetics line-so reasonable your pocket it won't crunch.

Although the drug products are in Japanese label
There's something you can find for yourself or for your table
"Though JAS stands for Japanese Asian Specialty
No matter who you are you'll find something for you with no difficulty.

It's really worth the trip-it's another hidden treasure
Come in at your leisure-shop for your own pleasure
Sample what you've bought and you'll come back again
If you have to come by car or by a subway train.

6-7-00

"JUSTICE FOR SALE?"

why are they acting so surprised about leaders in the borough picking
                        candidates for judgeship
judges picking special lawyers with a mere hand grip
since we voters don't know the candidate we go along with our party
their lawyers get first pick to manage and share in fees of foreclosure that
                        can be hearty
you never know what's going on till someone blows the whistle
because they feel they didn't get a fair share - they're waiting for dismissal
even though this is clearly wrong - it is not illegal
we have to end patronage - break up the cozy circle and watch them like an eagle.

1-7-2000

"KEUR N' DEYE"

It seems to me in Brooklyn - Fort Green's where its at
I wrote about "Carol's Daughter" now Keur N'Deye is all of that
There's several African restaurants in this vicinity
Only one to satisfy your masculine and femininity.

The warm dining room is decorated in batiks with an animal motif
Look around and drink Bissap sorrel as an aperitif
The menu is Senegalese - wholesome simple cuisine
Served on large dishes with earth tones of the terrine.

You're welcomed as if you're in their home as a guest
See people with palms raised as their food is blest
People dressed in suits, slacks and African attire
Will only enhance your tastes as you seek what you desire.

Yassa guinaar (lemon chicken) popular and savory
A dish that's been around way before slavery
To mute the lemon tang-onions, peppers and rice they serve
Fish couscous or lamb mafe for those with a little nerve.

Thiou Kandj a sipakhe-chunks of okra with large shrimp
The aroma and the smell is enough-and on portions they don't scrimp
The coconut pecan cake is a just dessert
So leave room - so you can open up your skirt.

Remember it's the main courses that makes this a must
Come in, see for yourself and by the tastes you'll believe in my trust.
With everything I've said you'll know they care
So whenever you hear the name-smile and say "I know-I've been there.

5-7-00

Let them decide

Sometimes I wonder have we done our kids more harm than good
Books that have been banned which we read when we could
Little Eva and Topsy in Uncle Tom's Cabin
Making us look dumb because of the color of our skin.
(Talking about Topsy it was a part I played
cause I was the only black in the advanced 6th grade)

lil' Black Sambo realizing how fast he ran
to make the butter-how fast we run now-if we can
from the law or to a better life protecting our family - the children and the wife.

What we read about in our school days
Give them something to compare to as they go their separate ways.
How will our kids know how far writing has advanced
Let them choose what to read, make a choice - take a chance.

To them it might be comical - not a feeling of despair
But at least they'll have the chance to read and compare
Give the individual family or child the right to choose
Reading any book is not a minus but a plus-what have we got to lose?

9-3-00

'Light'

I talked to a friend just last night
A friend who has gradually lost his sight
I thought of Genesis 1:3 when God said "Let there be light"
If I had never seen - would I know the difference between day and night?

It happens every morning - the miracle of light
From dark to gray - to even bright sunlight
Some people have lost their physical eyesight
But see more clearly by a new spiritual light.

When you see or know it's the dawn of a new day
New opportunities, joys and responsibilities that will come your way
Do you appreciate the beauty you see in a face?
Bloom of a flower, bird in flight going from place to place?

Later today, the sun will set only to rise tomorrow
It will wash away all things - be it joy or sorrow
It will happen regardless of the date we give this day
Until your final sunrise - when to God you're on your way.

1-10-00

LOVE

There's many forms of love and sometimes we lose one
By death, divorce, break-up or relocation and their gone
When one has gone remember - that one you can't replace
That particular one - the one with a smiling face.

There's always an opportunity to love anew
It doesn't just happen - it's a choice made by you
When you're alone - remember you can choose
Build or deepen an existing one - what have you got to lose?

Give love to your family, friend, co-worker or a neighbor
To give love it might take your time and a little labor
There's some risk involved even in a platonic form
Making yourself vulnerable is really part of the norm.

To create more love in your life - how do you start
Be a good listener, practice tolerance and listen to your heart
Respect rights and opinions - take an interest in others
Reach out, speak out and converse with sisters and brothers.

Don't wait for someone to approach you - be active
Choose to give love and life will become more attractive
Then watch the ancient adage come true for you
What you sow - you'll reap and love will start from you just being you.

2-10-00

MONEY FOR THE MILLENNIUM

A new year, new millennium and new dreams
Goals, ambitions, resolutions - its not what it seems
Saving money is usually top of the list
Sometimes labeling us as having a real tight-fist.

Besides investing wisely there is an easy way
So heed some of these things that I have to say.
Take a book, you read it once - Go to the library - why buy
If your credit card charges an annual fee and the rate is high
Ask to have it waived or each month pay in full
With your long-distant calls also be real careful
Use only your banks ATM to avoid and extra service charge
Use generic brands, keep your car serviced and battery recharge
Use public transportation whenever it is possible
Keep the house heat low whenever it is plausible.

Pay your bills on time - never be late
These savings may seem small and really not so great
But every penny saved is a penny earned
So, we've started the new millennium with some things we have learned.

1-9-2000

My paper — doll family.

When I was little-never had a sister or a brother
Mom had died, no one to play with but grandma - her mother
She having a bad heart, a husband and 3 sons of her own
Had little time to play with me-when she finally did sit down.

Today I saw in a magazine - a family I held dear
I could talk to them, for them and they were always near
I could change their clothes, dress them as I wished I could
They were the main family and friends of my early childhood.
Yes! It was my paper-doll family of the past
Children of today only play with things that are telecast
They'd think this is corny cause they wouldn't talk back
Have no remote or parts that break or maybe even crack.

Did you have a family that you kept in a box
You'd talk to them so long-you were called a chatterbox
If you did maybe you'll also remember-you were never a lonely one
Whenever you wanted company you could be with someone, anyone or everyone.

YOUR PAPER-DOLL FAMILY.

12-15-00

"REMEMBER"

Favorite foods I had when I was young
That seemed to wake up the senses of my tongue
Devil Dogs and chocolate milk was my favorite lunch
Apples, oranges, grapes and raisins were the things to munch.

Codfish cakes from dried cod - more fish than potatoes
Our standard Friday dinner - with whole stewed tomatoes
Swedish rye bread — a rye with a sweet taste
Covered with peanut butter, oleo, or Fluffo - nothing went to waste.

Nothing like fluffy dumplings in a chicken fricassee
Vegetables from the garden and all cholesterol-free
In summer-lemonade, iced tea or mixed together for a punch
Too late for breakfast-corn fritters and fried smelts for an early lunch.

Did you eat any of these things?
Does it bring back memories with a special zing?
Hm-m-m-m-m.

9-24-00

"SPEAKING FROM THE GRAVE"

If I was a mother who had lost my life
After being a loving mother and a wife
I'd be turning over in my grave
Knowing that God-my precious possession had saved.

And now the country I was running to
Wants to send him back — after all that I'd been through
Back to what I took my chances to get away from
Was now using my son — like a TV sit-com.

If his father was so great — would there have been a separation?
From his dad and my country would I be seeking liberation?
Have I lost my life — was it all in vain
Can't you see I was trying to give my son-one with less pain?

Yes! A father's love is great-but with a whole new family
Another woman raising another woman's child is no bowl of chili
Then have you asked my son "what do you want to do?"
If you did I'm sure you'd understand what was between us two.

How many times-going by the law-children sent to a biological
Were mistreated, abused and even killed-is that logical?
I hope the country I was running to will never have to say
That boy would have been alive if we had only let him stay.

4-8-00

"JUAN SAYS"

You've heard from my ex — from the grave
Now hear from me-what do you think I gave
I never knew she was gone with my son
Until I read in the paper and knew he was the one.

Why do I have to go to Miami to prove my love
He's blood of my blood given to me from the Man above
He's being used as a pawn by United States and Cuba
He'd have already been home-if he was from Haiti or Aruba.

Yes! I'm afraid of these strangers-not one of them a friend
For my wife, my other son-no one to help me try to defend
I want to feel good about myself and my family's situation
Let my son go — rid him of his infatuation.

With the worldly things and his cousin trying to be a mother
Let me take him to his grandmothers, stepmother and brother
The money being spent to close blocks or cordon off an airport
To overtime for police and discussions in the court
Could be better spent-I'd like you to know
Just be realistic and let my son go.

4-8-00

"STREET NEWS"

Until I went to "Night of Stars Café" to spend time with L. Monique
I had never heard of Indio or Street News-isn't that unique?
I received a copy it was given to me free
I read "a paper for the homeless"-what's that to do with me?

I took it home and said — oh well I'll just scan it through"
After page one — my interest just grew and grew
Since I had met Indio — I started with the Editor's Note
I thought this is interesting — I like what he has wrote.

I began to read the stories-was I amazed
I thought this is going to be about "The Bowery Bum."
But here were writings from across the country and across the sea
Writings from old, young and from some-to drugs they had succumb.

I usually read my paper — tie it up — to recycle
But there were so many writings from J.R. to Michael
I'm keeping this "Street News" for a story to put to rhyme
I'll keep reading it — it may take a little bit of time.

      "Street News" and time — I have them both
      maybe I'll be a part of their 11th year growth.

10-12-00

Teacher shortage.

Here I go again - the kids want to know
What I think of - why our urban kids are slow
My biggest beef has always been of class size
No one person with 30 or more can really supervise.

How can they keep order and get their message across
With disruptive children who demand to run the show and be boss
When some who needs more help are sitting in the back
No one extra to help them keep up with the pack.

Some that get bored because they know all that
One teacher can't keep them occupied - she has no time to chat
With all of this - the salaries are real low
If they're qualified and get a chance to the suburbs they will go.

This to me is why to get good teachers it is hard
Correct these things - maybe they'll stay in our back-yard
If you are the best would you choose-a low-performing school
Teacher's shouldn't have a choice-motivation should be the rule.

Then you have the parents who can't help with the home-work
They don't know how or are too tired from their menial work
Poor attendance, no homework - to talk to a parent there's no chance
Honey, I would leave a city's system without a backward glance.

1-21-00

THE DAILY PAPER

The newspaper's a trusted friend
It arrives everyday on that you can depend
It tells you about people and events of the day
Government an international affairs and what they have to say
Sports, business affairs and comics for something light
All about the weather - sun rise and moon at night
Crime here, war there and people that have died
Sometimes it's not quite correct - maybe even lied
So what does that tell us - we need something more dependable?
Like the Holy Bible - more reliable and even recommendable.

7-20-00

"THE FIRST BIRTHDAY"

What are mother's of today doing?
Think of some of the things we are viewing
When I was young until 16-ice cream and cake was all you got
And Kool-Aid made in mama's biggest cooking pot.

The biggest event for the family was the christening party
Now it's the baby's first birthday that is hale and hearty
You invite children-all of them older-to play and eat
While your little ones watch-can't stand on their two feet.

A magician, rides for the kids and even a clown
That the birthday child doesn't know-what's really going down
Pizza, hamburgers and franks-he/she can't even chew
Soda, ice-cream and cake and a lot of ballyhoo.

Then don't forget the booze and hors d'oeuvres for the adults
If you're counting on presents-some are real insults
If you'd only had the family and the grands
You'd have gotten the best and it wouldn't have gotten out of hand.

Now everybody had a good time-but the birthday child
Whose been asleep for hours before the party got real wild
This is one party they'll not remember or have a clue
And you'll still be paying for it-when the next one's due.

9-5-00

The Junk Drawer

How many of you are like me - having a junk drawer
In the kitchen, garage, basement or even a little more
Mini flashlight, buttons, Krazy glue or foreign coins
Luggage keys, blank tapes or recipes for sirloins.

Every time I open the drawer to drop in something new
I tell myself, that's the next thing I am going to do
Things we don't want or need but unwilling to let go
Why do we keep it - tell me - I don't really know.

This year I've decided to adopt the one year rule
If I haven't used it, throw it out be it a utensil or a tool
Give it to a charitable organization, family or a neighbor
We'll get rid of all the clutter with a little bit of labor.

It will make it easier to keep tidy and clean
Give us an A-plus for fastidious hygiene
We'll put it in a bag - say "It's out of here"
So it won't be in a drawer for another year.

1-8-2000

"Time"

How many times have you heard some one say "I'm just killing time."
What a cruel thing to do for something that's so valuable
Time's to be cultivated - not murdered - that's a crime
It should not be wasted - but used - that's not arguable.

Sometimes we must relax and rest — but that's not killing time
It's using it for restoration be it day, noon or nighttime
If a fraction of the time we waste, we prayed or helped a friend
What a difference it would make when your day has end.

You may think I'm narrow-minded but the Bible's clear
In Eph. 5:16 be wise redeeming the time - with no fear
For its not true that we can make up for lost time
For it is gone forever - just like your very last dime.

SO USE IT OR LOSE IT.

4-3-00

THEY'R –R-R BACK

Last year I wrote a poem "They leave but come back."
Today I smiled when it's now published that it's a known fact.
They said 35% of unmarried women and 45% of unmarried men
Back for a lot of reasons and you parents say "Oh! What again?"
Why are all these people really going back
They have a good job but can only afford what they call a shack
Thanks to sky-high rent - you need a room-mate
If you're not a couple you can't afford to date.

Then there's divorced people who need a hand paying a bill
And God knows - don't have children then it's definitely all downhill
Parents feel you're not successful enough to live on your own
Children feel a stigma - thinking I'm going home and I'm grown.
There's the tendency to revert to acting like a child
Or to stop your parents from spoiling their only grandchild
Reviving arguments of leaving dishes in the sink
Or harping on what you eat or how much you seem to drink.

You know this is your parents home - their wishes to obey
The adult child feels restricted and afraid to disobey
Your mom says "your friend can stay overnight but not in the same room"
She's not comfortable with it - so you spend your week-end out-
                  Wherever or with whom.
Then there's the couple who come home-saving for a mortgage and a house
If they get too comfortable, looking begins to wane and you feel like a louse.
You begin feeling guilty but refuse to take a stand
Until you've had enough-now you MUST show your hand.

The trickiest is the divorced ones who come home with a child
You're expected to take care of the grands and some are a little wild
You feel you must take care of both-the adult feels an intrusion
Till one says enough - to move is the conclusion
To avoid such headaches have a talk at the outset
Even draw up a contract, put it all on paper - so you don't forget
Set a goal for how long this is expected to last
Expect them to pay rent and don't dwell on the past.

If its not a cultural thing to live with your parents
Take it as a temporary measure, compromise - so you never wish you hadn't.

Inspired by
Anne Field 2-20-00 Daily News.   3-12-00

"VOTING."

I've been voting since 1940 and never had a clue
I always thought the president was chosen by you
The Electoral College - automatically went to the favorite one
But this year's fiasco has made me think it's not true -HE WON.

I would have gone on until death with this assumption
If Al Gore hadn't made a challenge and used his manly gumption
Truly it wouldn't have been so noticeable
If it had happened in any other state it might have been permissible.
But in the one state where there is kinship
It seems so odd to be considered only a slip
That so many discrepancies have turned into a doubt
But don't despair - vote again - it will all check-out.

11-14-00

"WONDERFUL"

if there was reincarnation and you come back-what would you be
this was a question by my three sisters-over coffee they asked me
my single struggling sister said "I'd be a white woman's poodle riding in a
        luxury car."
Sister #2-"I'd be rich, make a lot of money and be a super-star."
Sister #3-"when I come back I'd be president and change things Near and far."
My answer was "I'd be a black woman." They all groaned and said "dah"

I'd come back with a mind fierce and sharp
With spiritual fault - I'd learn to play the harp
I'd have a smile that is warm-a body so divine
Honey, cinnamon, or chocolate skin-either would be fine
Whether young or old I'd have enough money
So I'd never have to say-"It's in the mail honey."
I'd be a sister to sister-wise when choosing a mate
Remember birthday's, anniversaries, and every important date.

I'd be able to cook greens, BBQ chicken, macaroni and cheese, cornbread,
peach cobbler and lemon pound cake all at the same time
Walk down streets-have compassion for the homeless yet know
When and how to sidestep an oncoming crime
I'd have subscriptions to Essence, Jet, Ebony, Black Enterprise.
Heart and Soul and the Wall Street Journal
I'd have love-internal, external, maternal, paternal, and even fraternal.

I'd have at least one diamond from the motherland
On my finger or my neck put there by my husband
Courage of Rosa Parks, voice of Ella, political voice of Ida Wells
Spiritual poise of Susan Taylor, business savvy of Oprah, write
Like Maya or Vanzant - my stories to sell
Whatever a person says or does wouldn't change my demeanor
I'd focus more on God - my soul would be much cleaner
So if reincarnation is real let me return as a woman that is black
My esteem would be high and I'd be glad that I came back

11-21-00

"YOU JUST GOT HERE"

People emigrate to better themselves-that's understood
Buy a house, get new property in a nice neighborhood.
But do you realize you have to keep up an appearance
There is no longer a landlord to call on to run interference.

You have to teach your children to respect yours and others property
To help then realize we're now living above poverty
Customs vary but good manners and respect never go out of style
Wherever you come from-nothings so easy as "good-morning" or a smile.

Homeownership means its yours-so keep it looking good
One bad house an the block-there goes the neighborhood
To some a roof over your head maybe all you care about
It didn't look bad when you bought it-so make a turnabout.

Try to make it better and to your neighbors be friendly
By living close to others try not to be unfriendly.
So if you've been here for awhile or just got here
Try to make it pleasant and let them know you care.

5-17-00

MY LIFE STORY

I've got friends from the Caribbean and the deep south
Telling how things were - so from the horses mouth
Here's my side –
From the time my mom died.

My Mom died in childbirth - I was the only child
I was on both sides the first grandchild
Her mother took me home and bought me up
So here's a bird's eye view of my life style close-up.

I lived in a big shack - I didn't know it then
Raised by grandma, grandpa and their three grown men
Lived most of my life in a big kitchen with a cold stove for heat
A stove we used even in summer - if we wanted to eat.

On the back of the stove a big kettle always sat
For the bath, dishes, clothes and all of that
People now talk about recycling saying that we ought 'ta
In my day we didn't call it that but we did it with the water.
We used a tin tub, took a bath, washed the clothes and then the floor
Watered the garden by throwing it out the back door.

For deodorant and toothpaste - baking soda was the thing
Used a kerosene lamp for reading, light and schooling
I took a potty with me when I went upstairs to bed
Come to think of it my uncles never did, guess they used the windows instead.

Sometimes your pee would freeze when it was very cold
Didn't know-thought this happened in every household.
Grandma had a bad heart - I learned to shop at seven
So I wouldn't have to take anything back - I was professional at eleven.

Grandpa was a street cleaner with a broom and cart
When a cerebral hemorrhage took him - it really broke my heart.
Feb. 10th , 1929 I cried for my possession
While white folks committed suicide for Wall St. and depression
Though grandma, uncles and aunts were dear
It's only grandpops day - I remember each and every year.

I learned to embroidery, clean , shop and sew
Grandma did all the looking - so that l didn't know
Went to work for the white folks at age thirteen
They taught me how to serve, set a table and do the silver clean
Make hospital corners on each and every bed
Made most of my clothes, by hand with needle and with thread.

At sixteen I met the man I thought would be all mine
He had a glib tongue and a real sweet-line
When grandma died I was 17 - I knew I was on my own
I married that man at 18 - feeling I was really grown.

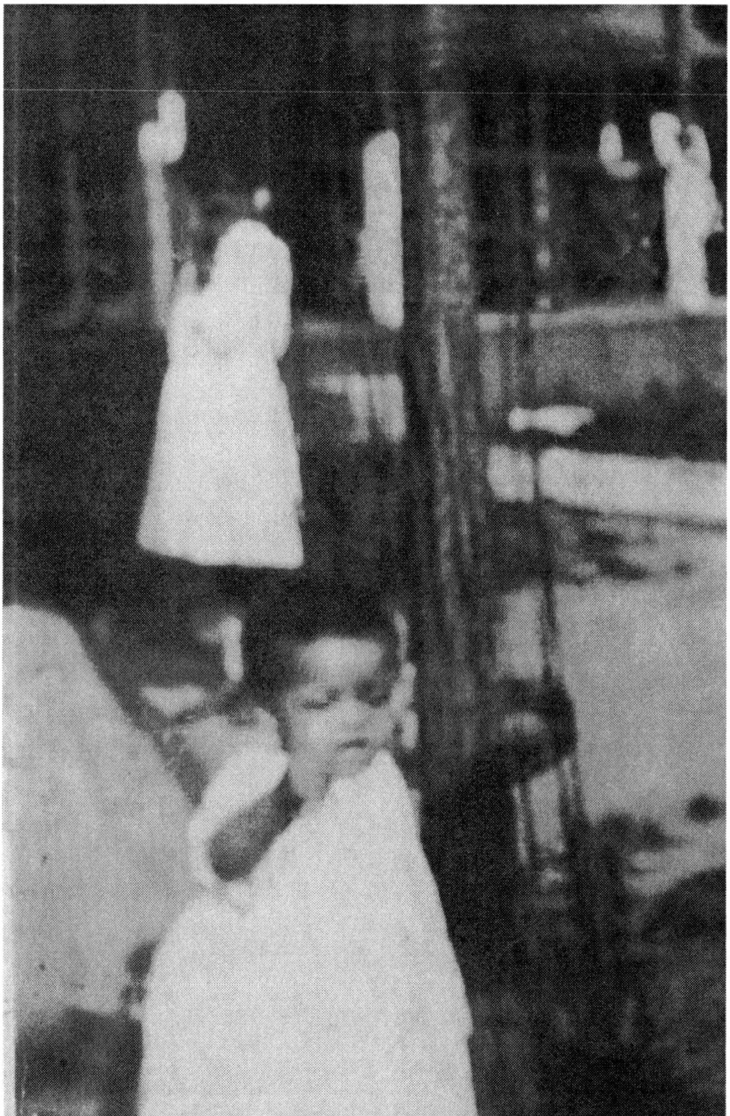

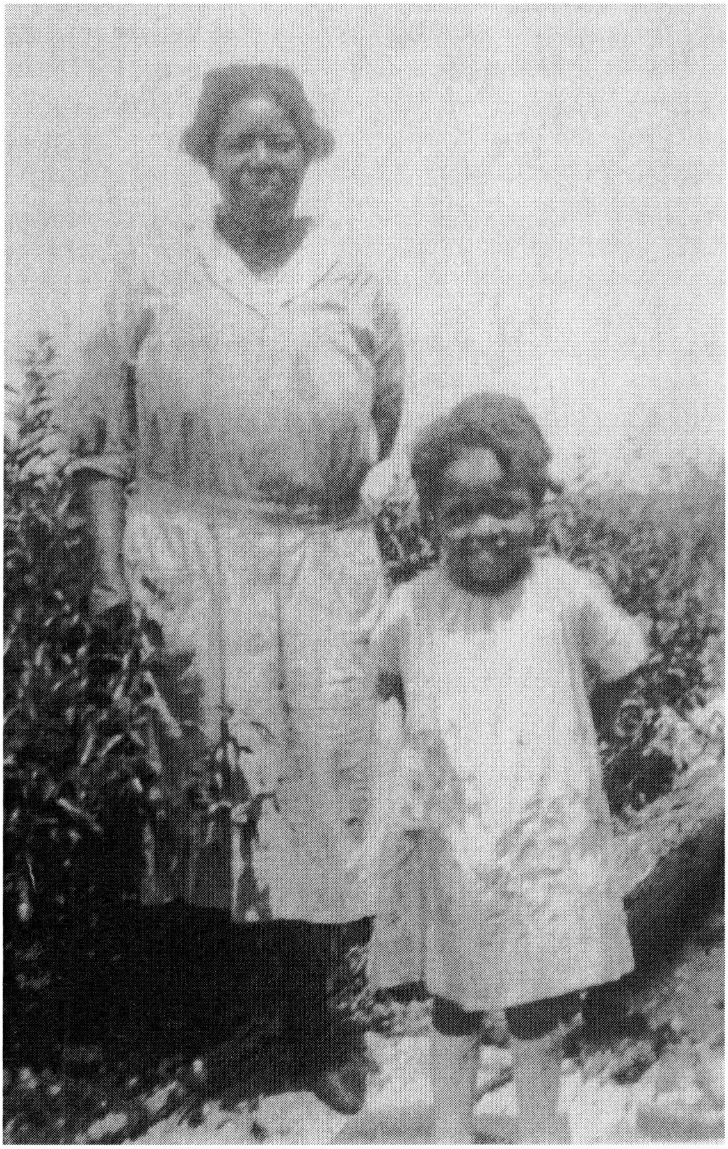

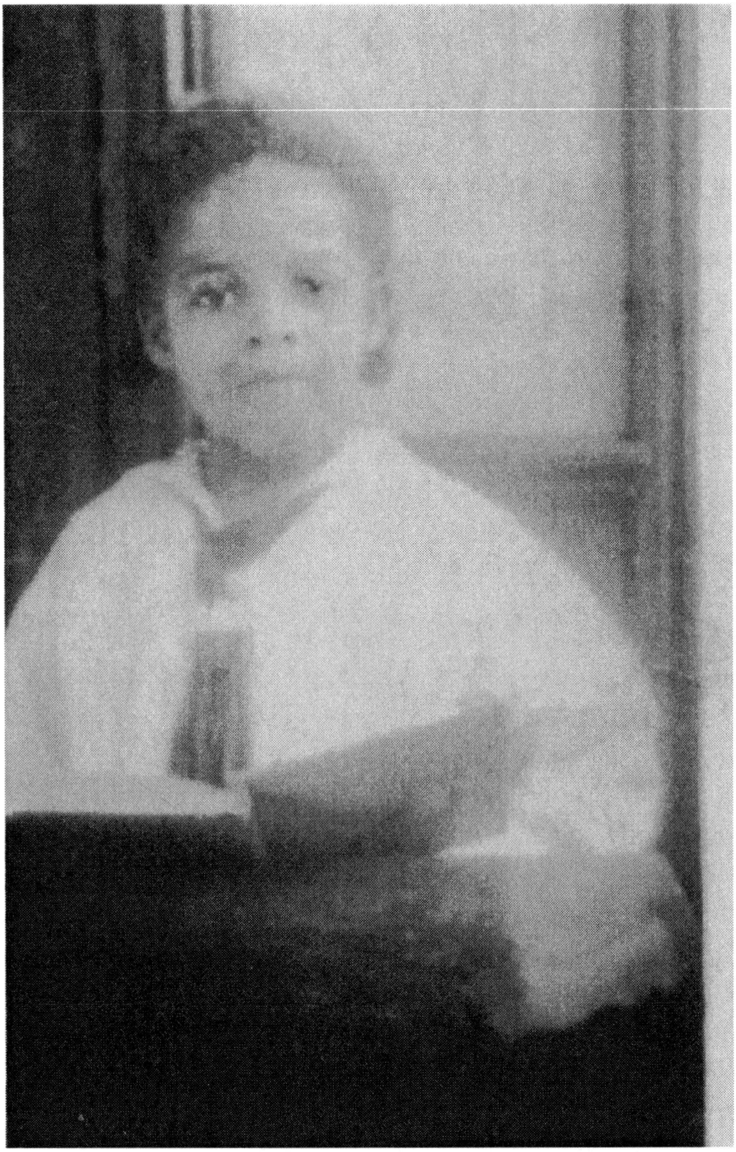

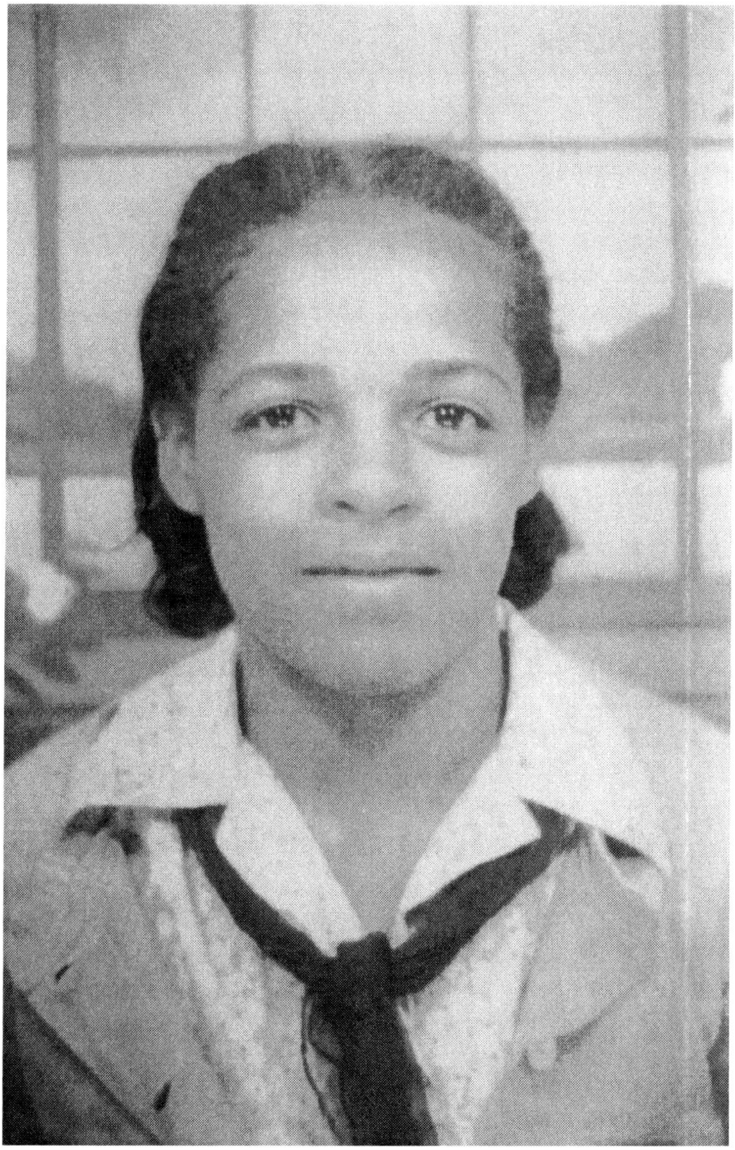

C.M.

Life with number one was no fun
He always made me feel that I was no one
He always threw in my face - he bought me into society
The main thing was never to create notoriety
He said in his life you shared your man
We'd argue cause I said "I don't think I can."

One day he came home with a dose of the clap
We didn't have penicillin so sulphur was on tap
Poor dumb me - he told me got it in church from the toilet seat
Until the Dr, talked to me - then I knew I had a cheat
I was 5 ft. 1 - she 5 ft. 10 without a doubt
But I went into the church and snatched the woman out.

I was told that was notoriety that you can't do
I said "I might be from the slums but to my man I'm true"
From then on we only fought at home
His poor parents if they had really known
So when he got killed I was very sure
I had to move on or back to being poor.

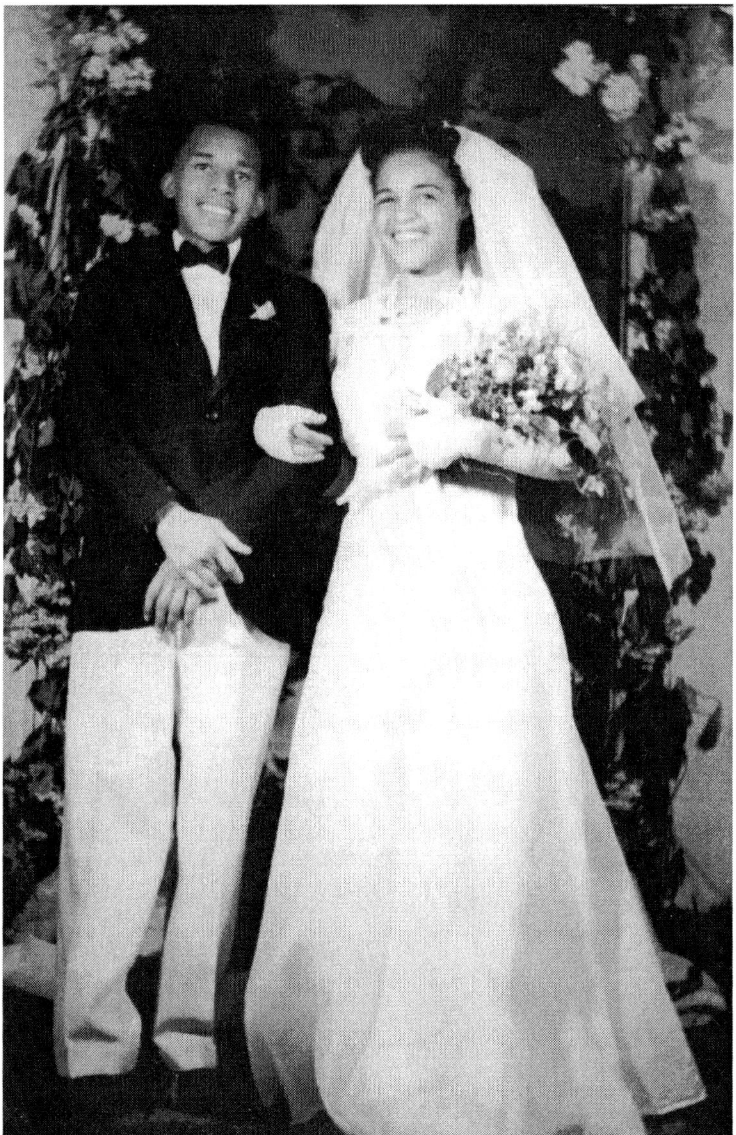

WISHING

When you were young did you wish for a specific thing?
Maybe at 5 or was it a toy for Santa Claus to bring
When I was 13 and all alone I wished for some one to love me
Not for someone whose favorite sentence was "what can you gimme?'
At 17 I wished for a baby I could call my own
An apartment with heat, hot water and maybe a telephone
They say be careful what you ask for you just might get it
I got those things - while I was ahead I should have really quit.
God gave me all of the above and then He took them back
I didn't understand so I questioned that.
I said "Lord I'm serving you - what am I to do
You've just taken a child from me - not one but two?"
But in a matter of months coming home from a revival
Two boys were killed and two were called a survival
One of those killed was the father of that kid
Then I knew right then God knew better than I did.
What would I have done with no family and two little ones
I know now He would have helped - since my life had just begun.
Being a young widow to show my enrage
I gave into the Devil - he took over with rampage.
Having no one to talk to or even to guide
I began to drink, stay out all night and even lose my pride.
I thought if I had a baby I would settle down
I set my hat for the preacher's son the cutest in the town
With the help of the Devil he wasn't hard to seduce
Even though he was going with someone pregnant that was no excuse
Through the stomach to his heart that's the way I went
With a vengeance I went after him till he became content.

T. H. S.

Her mother took him to court I stood by his side
In those days I looked the best so all of his boys lied
The judge said "Now that you have chosen your wife
In the army you will go - that will be your life."
After boot camp on furlough he came back
I laughed and teased him and nicknamed him "Sad Sack"
The old woman [her mother] put a curse on my only son
At 3 months a bout of pneumonia before his life begun
Almost lost him with spinal meningitis
Double mastoids, all kids diseases and osteomyelitis
He learned to get around with a cast on his leg
The doctors said he would never walk - never say never I said
They sent for his dad - gave him last rites
His grandpa came and prayed - left saying " It will be all right."
They said if he makes it to seven - he'll live to be a man
With all he went through I felt God must have a plan.
He did learn to walk although one leg was short
It never stopped him from doing anything once he was taught.
He then had a little sister - boy what a dream
She was so healthy it was to the extreme
Everything he'd had double of - she had none
She became his protector and would fight anyone.
Finally "Sad Sack" came home from the service
He didn't and wouldn't work and that made me nervous.
I did piece work - knitting boucle' suits for Leaf's
Hand-addressed envelopes at ½ a cent a piece
We drank beer and wine from morning to night
Had rent and card parties and stayed high as a kite.
When the kids were 6 and 7 - I had had enough
I had to leave my kids and that was really rough.
I went to my fathers and my Aunt Jean
Cut down on any drinking - my act I tried to clean
Started doing day's work - 80c an hour - trying to get upon my feet
But couldn't save a penny - had the rent and had to eat.
When I asked for a raise to bring it to a $1.00
They began to rant and rave and even to holler
That I was the best-dressed house worker on the Grand Concourse
    Did they think I was working to be a second-hand clotheshorse?

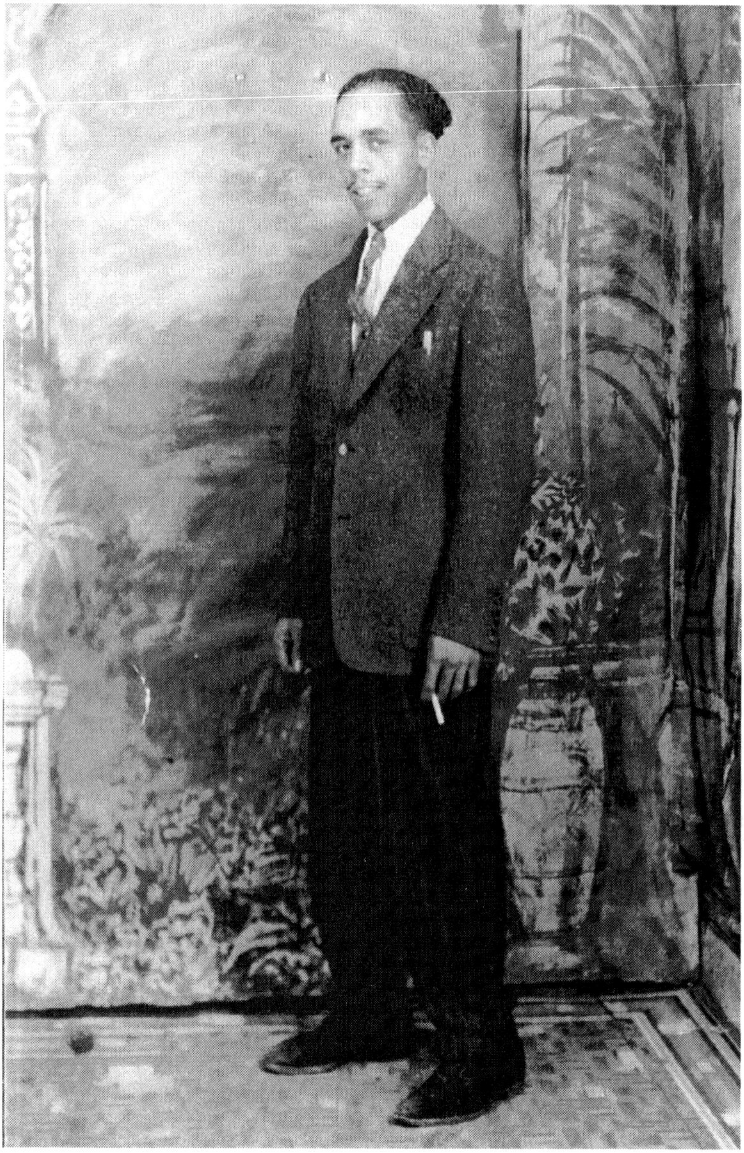

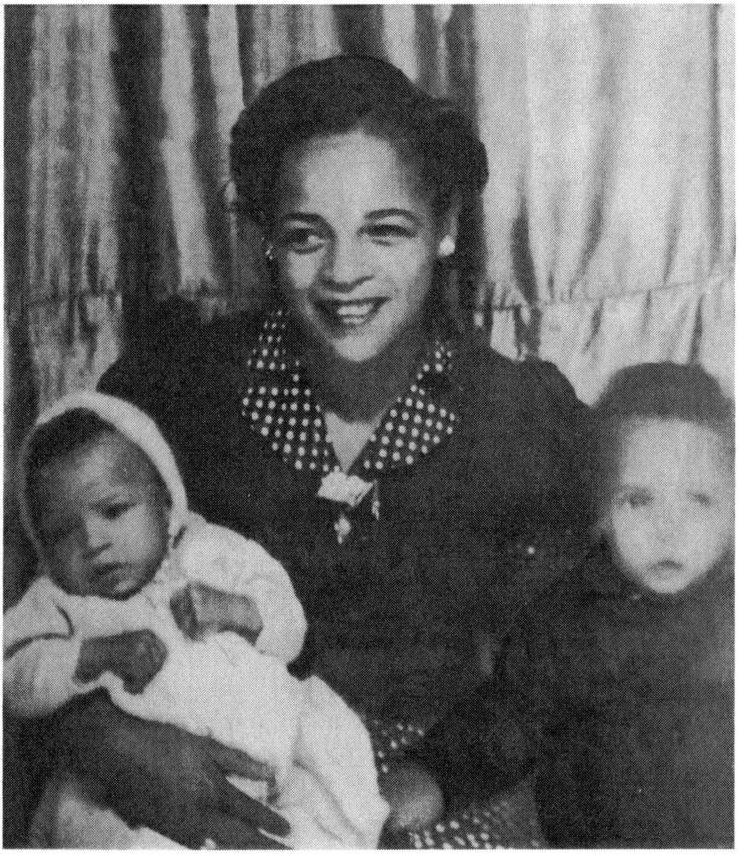

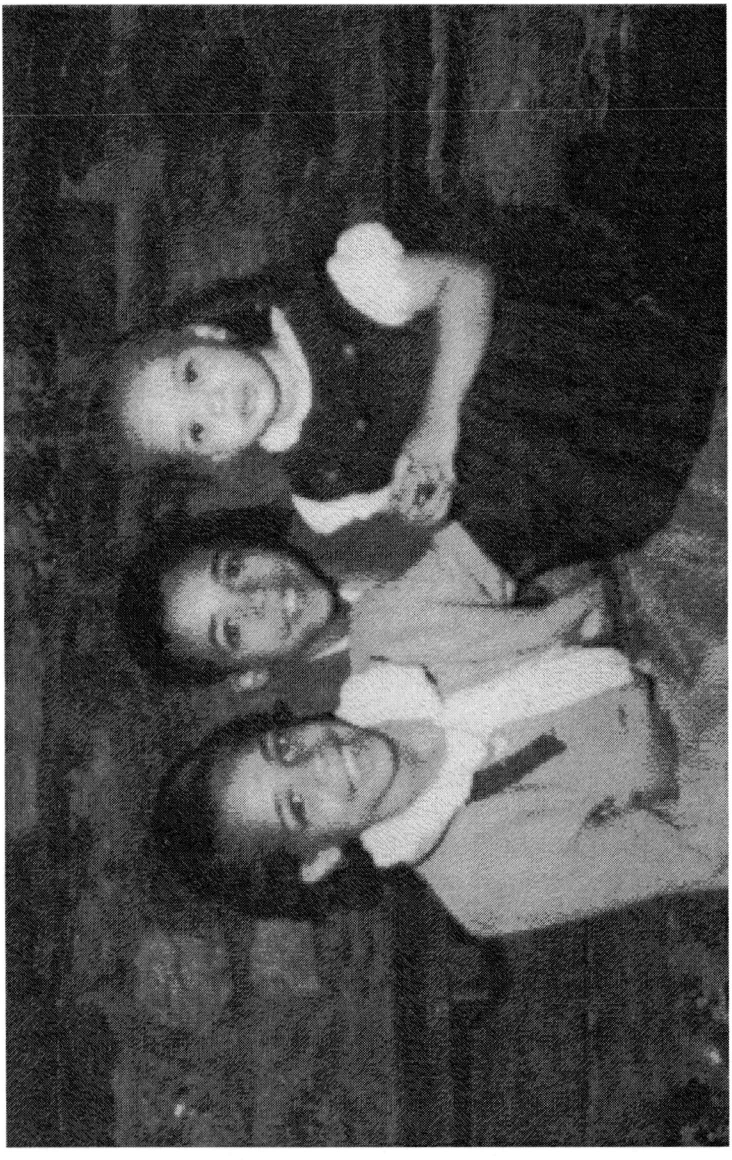

R. O. W.

When I left I went into Direct Mailing - cutting plates for magazines
It was like piecework - more you cut a bonus could be seen.
I took a test for the state - went into "State Insurance"
Kept both jobs - working 9 to 5 - 6 to 1 with strong endurance.
Then I met this man he had just cut his hand
He was living at home - a mama's boy - I didn't understand
After nine years - I found out I was pregnant
Now I really needed money cause I had an infant.
When I found out he was cheating - sent him back to his Mom
He said "I'm sorry" and I believed him - took him back - boy was I dumb.
He changed - yes he got worse so I decided it was time to go.
We moved all the things with a shopping cart - it was really slow
Over a mile there, put things in place - then a mile back
He never knew a thing was missing - we had a subtle knack.
One day my friends looking for me called. He said "She has flown"
Everything is gone but me and the telephone."
As you can see by now my choice in men wasn't very good
I'd been looking for love in wrong places from my child hood.

So my next man - speaking Spanish as she did
Rhonda picked him even though she was a kid
I never knew that I was that much older
Till he got hooked on drugs and became a free loader
Abusive, demanding and wouldn't hold a job
So here I go again - getting rid of another slob.

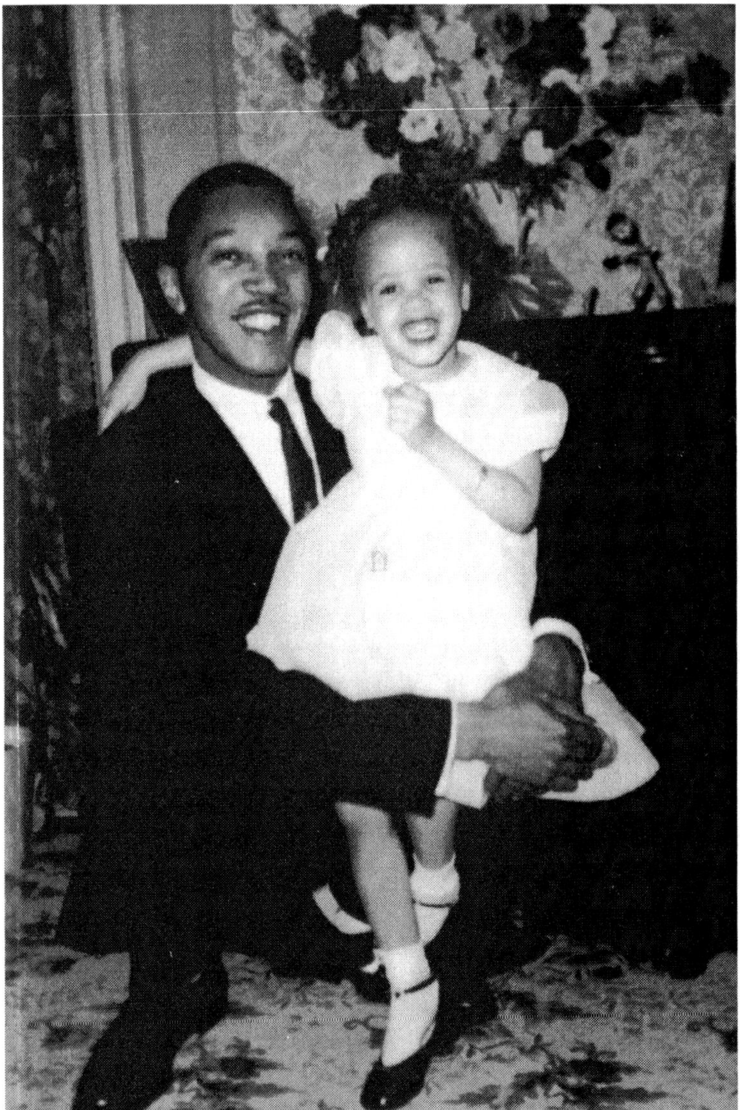

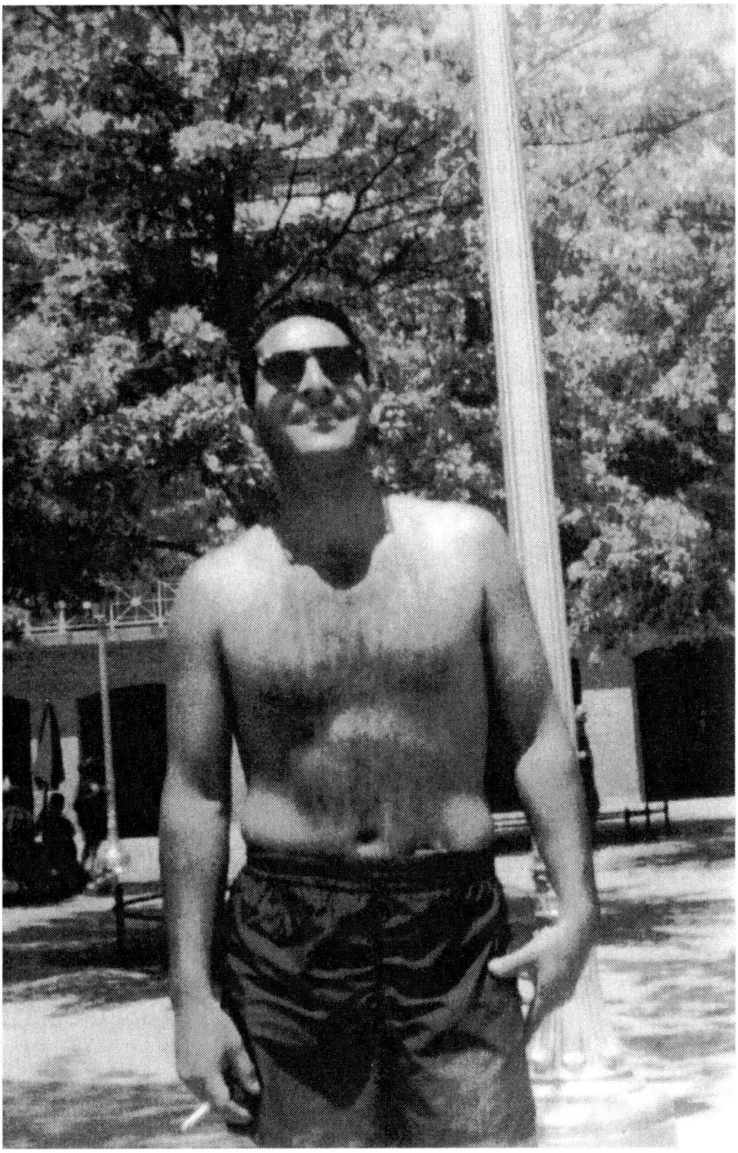

V.H.

I'm still working two jobs - the state and direct mail order house
They want to double my rent - I decide to buy a house
One of my friends cried said "you'll never make it"
With "Sad Sack" a G.I. Loan I knew I wouldn't quit.
I felt terrible - but I'm back to being wicked again.
I took him for awhile - then I had to let him go
He was more of a woman than you'd ever know.
The girls loved him being with me - they had nothing to do
He cooked cleaned, washed and did the ironing too
As for sex he could never pass the test
I went back to drinking heavy - to clear my conscience - I guess.

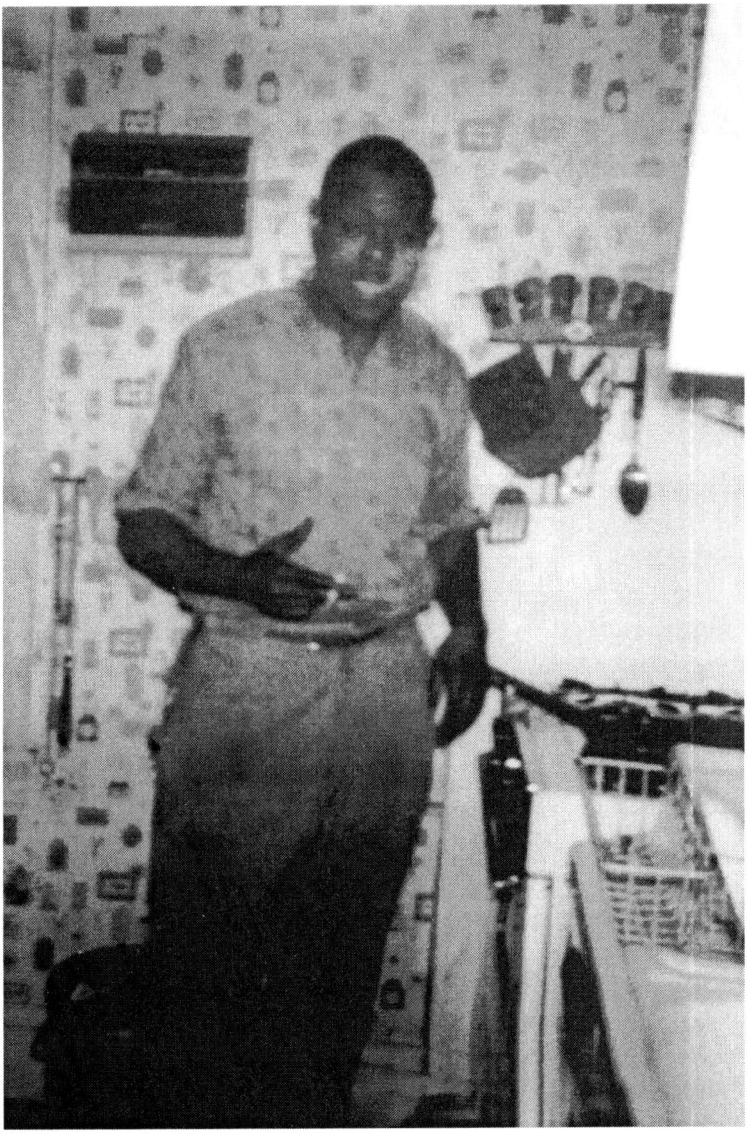

H. N. B.

After working two jobs for about five years
I decided to leave one "Told my friends I'm out of here."
I'm taking the postal test - get a job where there are men
Find one that will help me - so here I go again.

As I sat boxing mail feeling discontent
This cute little fellar swept my case - often and frequent
Every time he'd pass by he'd repeat this line
"I got the money if you got the time."
This was the beginning of a beautiful romance.
I figured this was my very last chance.

For five years we lived, loved in a drunken stupor
We thought our life was going to be super-duper
Finally on one sober occasion
He asked me to marry him - with a little persuasion.

All my friends, neighbors and family said "No"
But I said "Mind your business - I'll make it a go."
So I married him - deep down for the wrong reason
Drunk driving, 13 accidents I thought this was his fall of his season.

After we married he still acted like he was single
He said "I'm a virile man that needs to intermingle."
The guys he worked with would lie when I called for him.
I decided to leave the post-office I had to sink or swim.

I went back to working in insurance
A job I loved with love and assurance
It was perfect - I worked days and he midnight
Till one day I came home early and what a sight.

Glasses on the couch - woman in my bed
I was fit to be tied and I saw red
I was always taught - one doesn't crap where one eats
I told him "I'll never sleep with you again between those dirty sheets."

When he got to bragging and naming name after name
I figured it was over - like any other game
I moved out of his bedroom - our sex went down the drain
When one of his women died of AIDS that was the very last strain.

Now we live in the same house, not even like sister or brother
We see each other everyday but don't speak to each other
He's alienated all friends but two
Heineken beer and E. J. Brandy are the two that will do

He lives upstairs and I live down
Only when he's drunk do I know he is around
After 35 years and more
He threatens to leave and walk out the door.

February 14 - yesterday was his birthday
He celebrated it with his two best friends
Heineken and E. J. Brandy which was his way
To enjoy the day and his time to spend.

Today is the 15th - God has intervened
He's helped him home across that great ravine
With his two friends to help him on his way
At last he's found peace - on his last birthday.

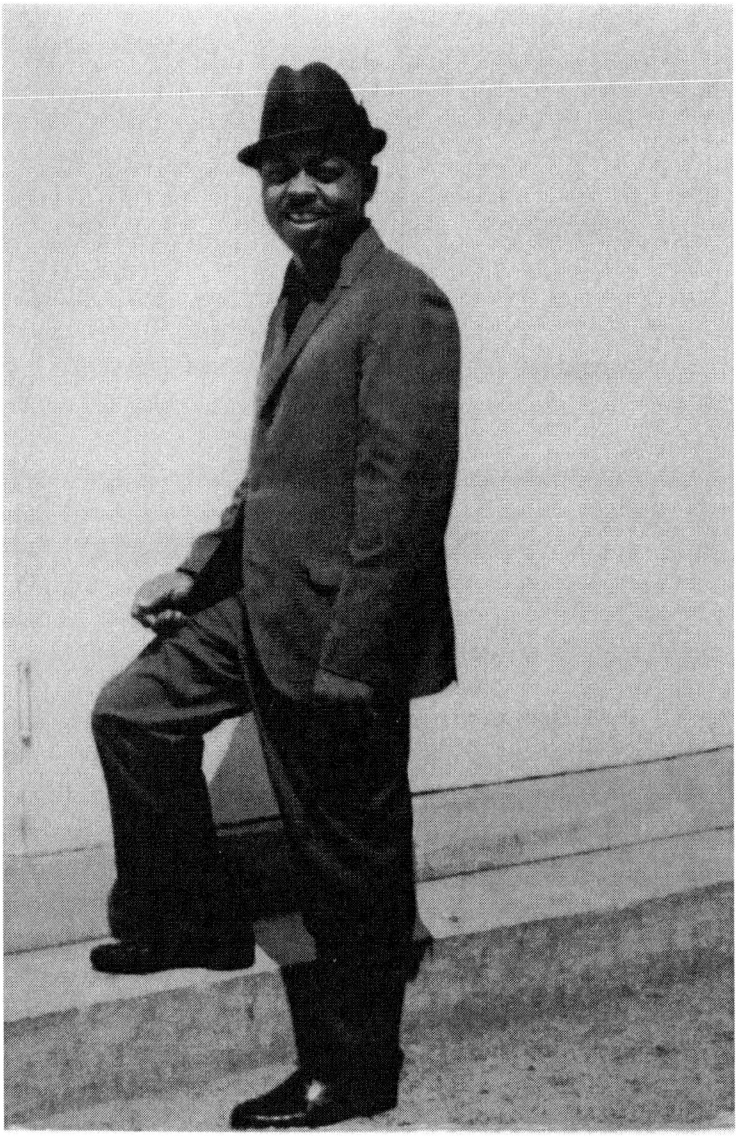

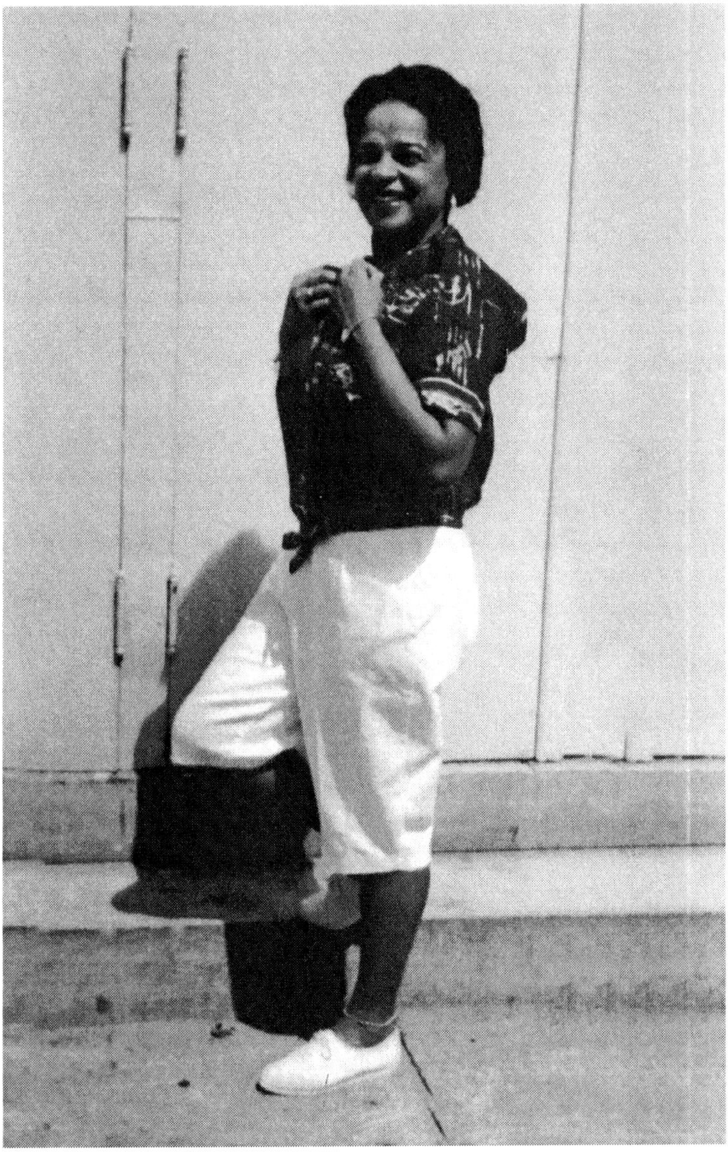

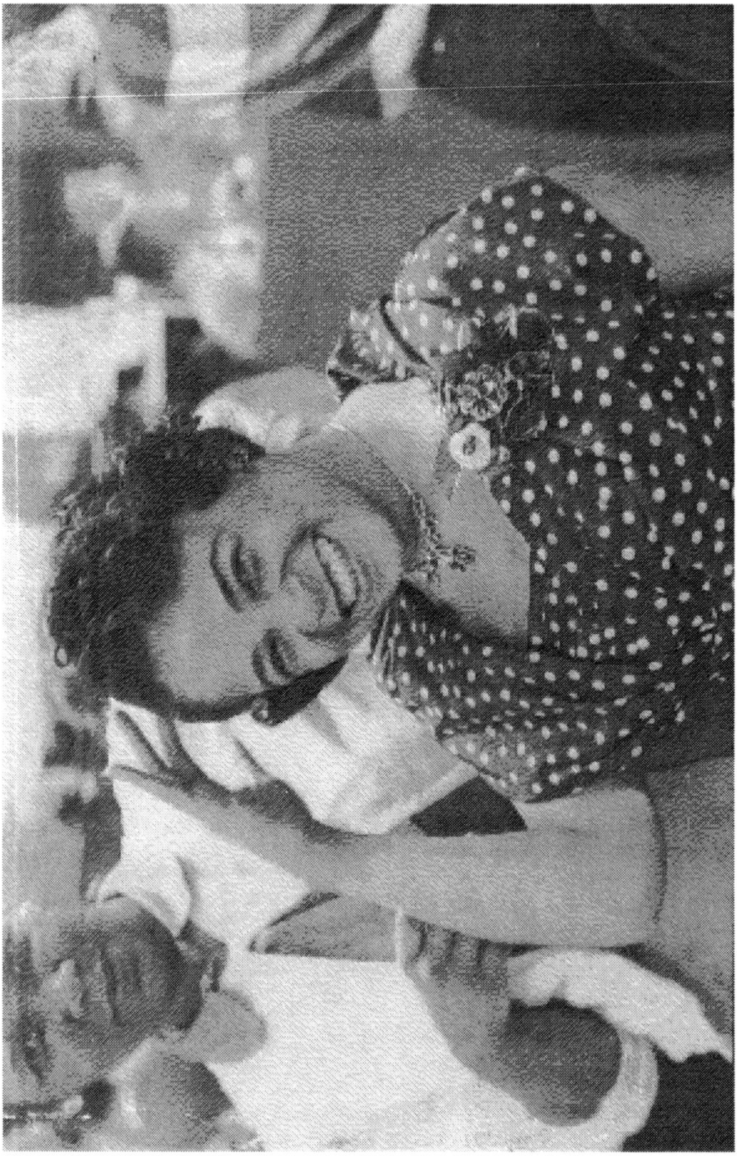

THE BROWN OSPREY

LITTLE OLD ME!!!

I'm old-go to bed early-up at three
Go to the bathroom, grab a pen and write my poetry
It might be about something of the past
Or about the TV program that I saw last
About the headlines that I read today
No matter what I write-it's got to be my way.
I go to bed with a collar on my neck
A brace on my hand-my body is a wreck.
My bed companions are a pen and a pad
Also Aleve cause the pain can get real bad.
But I look forward to the morning light
Thanking God-who watched me through the night.
I've risen to a day that is brand-new
I've got until 8 P. M. to do all I have to do
Then again-it's time to go to bed
To lay down my tired weary head.

GOOD NIGHT!!!

9-30-01

NO ONE TO TALK TO!!!

Now that I'm old and all alone
Can't talk to anybody even if I pick up the phone
All I get is a machine-press one-if you want to go ahead
I get so disgusted I hang up the phone instead.

If you hold on you hear a sermon or crummy music
I know you're not answering so I decide to click
Businesses from companies, insurance and banks
From pressing one to pressing six-say "No thanks"

To speak to a real person-press nine
Then wait a half-hour till they come on line
So you see-I spent all my morning all alone
And I never talked to a real person-even on the phone.

Inspired by Nancy O'Brien
Sun. Daily News
9-3-01

WHY!

Now that I'm older - I ask myself "Why do I drink?"
It's because sometimes I feel sorry for myself - I think
I really don't like the taste but I like the feeling
Of the warmth going down that is so revealing.
Sometimes I drink because I am really bored
Then I keep an going until I'm overboard
But if every things O. K. and on an even keel
I have my rum and coke with my evening meal.
I like to have company when I have a few
Or blame it on my bronchitis, even on the flu
But if you're there or if you're not
I don't really need a reason - if I want a shot.

12-17-99

"MY VIRGINIA JOURNAL"

7-12

I'm in Virginia Beach-this morning I started to walk
Only this time I walk with my daughter for a little girl-talk
We talk about the neighbors and the houses that are for sale
Of marriages that are flourishing and some that seem to fail.

7-14

today it was different as we looked above
looking at the work of an artist-who paints with lots of love
a perfectly blue sky and clouds so fluffy and white
that no one else could duplicate or get almost right.

7-15

I went to get my camera to try to photograph
Trees dancing in the wind that God had choreographed
As I look and see the rain skipping across the pond
It makes me realize it's from a world beyond.

7-16

Curtis scurried all week - working on an enterprise
It worked out swell-he finally gave Carole a surprise
A birthday party with her Grands and every Virginia beach friend
It was a big thing-almost two before it came to an end.

7-17

J.C., Teri and Nick arrived-I even stayed awake
Kept hoping J.C. would fry catfish and Teri bake a cake
We talked from day till night and even had a ball
Curtis took them house-hunting and shopping in the mall.

7-1 8

well I'm packing and gathering up my stuff
going home early-a wedding is cause enough
but because it's been so short-I'll be back real soon
ain't going to wait till next year for the month of June.

7-19

well I'm on my way home-today is the day
with Curtis and Nick - driving all the way
from Alabama, to Virginia to the asphalt jungle
it's good to be home-no matter how humble.

7-20-00

"MY WILL"

From my parents or husbands I never received anything
Everything I got was by my ingenuity or my working
Now I scrimp-thinking what can I leave my kids and be fair
How do I figure-what is their equal share.
So-sound in mind-I'm spending your inheritance
So you don't have to fight or worry and lose your patience
Nothing is due to you-I paid my dues when I gave birth
So it really doesn't matter how much you think I'm worth.
So you see there's enough to bury me
Liquor for the wake is here (so that's free)
All my bills are paid-that you will agree
All the rest is gone on a spending spree.

MOM

9-2-00

FAMILY ACQUAINTANCES AND FRIENDS

BARBARA

I have a friend I like in actuality
But her weakest point is her punctuality
If she gives you a time be it 7, 8, or 9
Sit, relax and have a drink or take time to dine.

She will show up - all out of breath - rushing like mad
She'll give you her biggest smile - shake her head and say "traffic's bad"
But with that beautiful smile how could you not forgive
You know she'll be late again as long as you both shall live.

To get you there she'll even manage to get lost
Will add to the delay at a minimal cost
When she gets you there she'll say "They didn't start without me."
Truthfully they couldn't because she's usually the emcee.

LOVE YA BARBARA.

3-20-99

BARBARA AND TONY

To Barbara and Tony together as one
Today your life has just begun
Together a beautiful couple you make
Just like the pair on your wedding cake.

May you two be happy and live a good life
You a loving husband - you a loving wife
With those rings the bind has been tied
You two will work together from now on side by side.

The "I do's" have been said - you're now a newly-wed
It's time to go home - time to go to bed
You'll wake up in the morning tired and worn-out
Now you're definitely Mr. And Mrs. Bethea without a doubt.

Good-luck but remember it takes more than luck
You have to work at a marriage like you do for a buck
It's not all give or not all take
You can eat it and still have your cake.

BUT IT TAKES WORK

Love ruth bell 11-20-99

"BIG BROTHER WAYNE"

you know the saying, "Be careful what you say and do!"
you never know who you'll meet - when, where or who
yesterday I met a man - I came to drain his brain
he was a big Teddy-Bear named Big Brother Wayne.
In the course of conversation I found out he knew my "grand"
The one who started me writing - so you'll understand
How I got to know him - he was teaching a class
His information was superb-two hours went too fast.
I came home told my "grand" I'd met Big Brother Wayne
She was in awe-acting like she'd gone insane
We talked about him and I did agree
That he's a big help to her and to me.

So if ever you see anything by "Brother Wayne" you're in for a treat
Go wherever he is-in a suite, at a meet or on the street
You'll like him and if you listen-you'll learn a lot
I'm glad I took his class-learning things I knew not
"Big Brother Wayne" I wish you more success and fame
when I publish-I'll be glad to your workshop I came.

THIS IS TO YOU!

Ruth "Ma" Bell
5-20-01

"BILL"

well - Bill - they still got you in the hot seat
you were labeled - a lying, two-timing cheat
I don't blame you lying - I'd be like "Shaggy's " song
Swearing "It wasn't me" if it took all day long
I always felt that you were set-up - it was a plan
I only blamed you-not remembering safe sex-although you were 'THE MAN'.
Now about Rich and your brother too
You have to do - what you have to do
If you can't help a friend, relative or neighbor when you're "THE BOSS"
When can you? It's done - it's over-live with the chaos.
Because you're still young-these are small hurdles in your life
So only worry about pleasing your daughter and your wife.

2-20-01

"BILL"

For 10 million dollars what does a publisher expect?
The media's told it all-stepped on your self-respect
What can you write or say that we don't know
That we'd be willing to pay out our hard-earned dough
They say it won't be published until 2003-it's true
By then I guess everything you say will be all brand new.

8-25-01

LEROY COMRIE ! ! !

Movie stars have roasts
Ordinary folks have toasts.
Tonight we're here to toast Leroy
Did you know him when he was a boy?
Well ! he was born in Jersey City-dubbed American first generation
So from Jamaica to Jamaica this is a time for celebration.
He came to Queens at four and he's still around
Brick Town and Cambria Heights being his stomping ground.
At Bridgeport University-politics became part of his life.
In 1990 he asked Marcia Moxam to be his lawful wife
He took a hobby-photography-made it a profession
But always remembering politics-his one complete obsession.
With all of this he still had times for fun and games
FUN-GAMES - Liana and Benjamin are their names.
St. Alban the Martyr-he's a lifetime member
Attending his church from January to December.
Cheering him on - Dad gone-but his mother
Also in his corner-Ronald-his one and only brother.
With Star Trek and Science Fiction he is a fanatic
With wonderful friends [mostly women] he's still Democratic.
They say "he can't buy one of anything."
Good for us-in office-he'll ask for more of everything.
"No more room here" Marcia said
How about Gracie Mansion next-room for all his stuff instead.
Since August Nineteen Hundred Fifty-eight
We are here now to congratulate
YOU-Leroy who has come a long, long way
In to the council-you can talk for us - have your say
A kudo for you-for us a fantastic win
We knew you'd be the one for us-as we voted you in.
So CONGRATULATIONS Leroy
Do your job and enjoy
Through your hard-labors-know this was meant
From your family, friends and workers we're with you 110 percent.

CONSTELLA

I went to Boston and I had fun
Reading poetry to an audience of one
Mother Laymon was her name
Glad she was there to visit-glad I had came
She was born in Georgia-I in New York
We found we had a lot in common as we began to talk
We both had become widows about a year ago
She was loved-she missed her husband
With me I don't think so
If I loved Constella-I'd have a ball with sister Ruth
She sounds like my kind of person-if you want the truth
I met Heather and John-a really loving pair
Can't describe them-meet them-really be there
I promised Constella-next time I'd bring a spicy one
To read just for her-not for her daughter-in-law or son.

11-3-01

DEVYN

Devyn you've been my inspiration
I talk of indigestion or of constipation
You talk of daily things - things that's in the news
I talk of house parties or low-down dirty blues.

Put us together - you'll get the whole picture
Some of the past, present and future
Your words are affluent, fast and clear
My words are slow with memories dear.

You say things I don't understand but
You take the time to explain I listen,
I smile the best that I can and
Sometimes the dark shadows fade.

Sometimes you talk real fast but you get your message through
So I'll just keep on listening - cause I believe in you.

Jan. 1999

EDDIE

Today is Kwanzaa - that's not why we're here to celebrate
We're here to help Lorraine honor - her adoring mate
He and his wife I met last year with an open arm
His big smile said "Welcome" with all his friendly charm.
He's not as loud as Curtis but can stir you up
As he sneaks his digs in - his eyes really light up
Not as quiet as Mickey or as subtle as Dupree
He'll show you a good time-'cause with Lorraine's money it's free!
No matter how you find him - he's good to have as a friend
If you need him to help, or make a drink, on him you can depend
If he's in New York City or in Virginia Beach
Call him - he'll be there, for he's not hard to reach!
HAPPY BIRTHDAY, EDDIE ! ! ! !

FRANKIE

Today we lost a husband, brother or a friend
He was one who really set a Landrine trend
He always had a smile and his eyes would light-up
He always had a hug as he really came close-up.

Ask him a question he'd answer "I haven't got a clue"
But he made you feel welcome - like he was glad to see you
He never said anything about anybody that was detrimental
He'd just do his little dance that was cute and sentimental.

His words of endearment were "You big dummy"
He'd rub his head, smile and pat his tummy
Laugh at you and ask for another beer
In parting he'd say "Gotta go see ya hear".

As sick as he was I never heard him complain
He'd say "What's the use - what have you to gain?"
Frankie now that you've gone to finally meet the rest
Look down on us and we'll remember-again "God took the best."

From Teeny, Sugar and sisters four
We all know - you don't hurt anymore
Now that you're safe in the hands of God
Show Him how you used your fishing rod.

FAREWELL FRANKIE.

3/7/99

HILLARY

First you ask why not Rudy - he's from New York
He's so demanding, he wants to rule the cops, schools and even where you walk
He's already been accused of misconduct with his staff
Are we to go through another Clinton thing - do you think we're daff?
We've had a peek in his closet - you know more is there
Where there's smoke there's fire - if not it's really rare.

Now with Hillary - a hint of an honest answer "I need this for ME"
It's not about N. Y.'s working women, children, health care or education - ME is the key
The best thing she's ever done was to have Chelsea
She wants our sympathy for her husband - we are angry
Do we give her a seat in year 2000 as a Senator?
As a reward for having a pig, a liar as her conspirator

But to me she's the better of the two evils
But to elect her will start a new batch of upheavals
So do we want to elect a man who wants to be a dictator
Or a woman whose only credit is being an "administrator".

June 1999

"KUDOS TO INDIO"

I rode home with Indio from Manhattan into Queens
He shared with us his life - from drugs to livable means
He talked about his dealing, his wife and children four
How he'd slept in doorways or on a concrete floor
You see even the best of us can be homeless too
That's why he works so hard to help see some one through
He's the typical example of - done that and been there
No matter how he hurts-you need him-call him he will always share
Share his savvy, compassion and what you want to know
To help you stand on your two-feet and even make some dough.

12-8-00

LIBERTY MUTUAL ! ! !

Have you ever called 848-2727?
"Hello - Liberty Mutual - we open at 11."
You say "I'd like to make an appointment-when can I come in."
Answer: "of course-you're overdue-where have you been?"
Then you meet Rose, Arlene, Angela or Jhashive-once in a while
No matter how busy they are - you'll always get a smile.

Now Dr. Passarelli - a doctor that's protective
Keeping you alive is his main objective
If you had hypertension before you came to him
He keeps trying everything to get you trim and slim
Pressure 144 over 90 he has a fit
Saying "Let's try to get it down a little bit."
He says cholesterol should be 3.5 no more than 5.5
He wants it at the lower - so he tries - so you can stay alive.
He tells you when you leave "Any problems immediately call me."
You see - they take an interest - Liberty Mutual's the place to be.

3-6-02

MIKE MATARAZZO !!!

Have you ever met a man you'd be proud to call son?
Michael Matarazzo-to me-he is the one.
I met him when I became my church photographer
As I bought my pictures in - he became my philosopher.
It was years before I realized he wasn't well
By his actions and his smile I could never tell.
Liberty One Hour Photo-he is the owner
With kind-hearted mature and customer service-he's a donor
Not only to his customers but to *N. Y. F. A. C.
Loving to take pictures-he gives his service free.
Ask Andrew Bauman how great he is
Taking pictures of autistic children - he really is a whiz.
The kids love him-they think-"He's one of us."
He plays, hugs and to one and all makes a fuss.
He attends all the games of Ozone-Howard Little League
He's said to be a good boss by every single colleague
The fire department and the police know he is a pal
Asking for help or a hand he answers "I shall"
I know his mom and family must be proud
So to all of the above-I proclaim out loud
I'm glad to have you as a friend
Kudos to you until the very end.

*N.Y.F.A.C.
{New York Families for Autistic Children}

Ruth "Ma" Bell
10-23-01

MONICA

What a reputation for a young woman to carry
Of being "THAT" woman - no proud man would marry
Of being the "sucker" of the top man in our land
Her face on every TV or on every news stand.
As she passes by - all the men will look and smile
Thinking of her position and of her style
Was it a sincere act or only for a job
A job she didn't even get but the handle of a slob.
Who keeps a dress that's dirty for over a year?
Or keep copies of letters you sent to some one dear
No one would do that unless you had a plan
To embarrass the First Lady or the Head Man in the land.

Jan. 1999

OLA

Lots of things you do for me I appreciate
Yet some things you do - I really hate
When you tell me over and over when to drink the water
I get enough of that from my grands and my daughter.

When you go on and on it really makes me sad
To think - you think I can't remember what I had
Sometimes I don't - it really is so true
But when you keep repeating - I get mad at you.

I know you're used to bossing Victoria and Liz around
But treat me like a grown-up you can't turn around
By just suggesting, not demanding what I should do
It will make me feel better about listening to you.

9-11-99

"MY FRIEND"

I have a friend - her emotions show in her face
No matter who she's with - no matter what the race
She has no patience - known to pace the floor
Looks out the window - even waits at her front door
When she's upset, tired of waiting-her eyes flash fire
If she's hungry - God knows-her hormones go haywire
But if you are one in need of a friend
She'll be there and yours until the bitter end.

11-16-00

OTIS !!!

Went to an 80th birthday and we had fun
Wife, children, grand-children and even a great grand-son
It was in Virginia Beach at a place called "Yesterday"
Food served superbly any way you'd say
A photo cake served-made by "The Sugar Plum"
Drinks were ordered from lemonade to Barcardi rum
A picture was presented of his humble Georgia roots
Where he learned to fish and he learned to shoot.
A plaque reminding him of his shooting and his fishing
A lifetime of 19 autos from 1940-isn't that astonishing?
Married to Etta Mae Sparks for 58 years or more
All of us here celebrating his fourscore.

HAPPY BIRTHDAY OTIS —GLAD TO BE HERE
WE"LL DO IT AGAIN—SAME TIME NEXT YEAR.

For Otis Lee Jackson

1-01-02

RUTH

People ask me where I'm from
My accent is profound
Harlem hospital was my birthplace
New Rochelle my stomping ground.
I've always been defiant - learned to stand on my two feet
Started working at 13 to earn my bread and meat
Got married at 18 for only a short time
God took him home - while he was in his prime.
This was the beginning - the story of my life
How I became a lover, mother and a wife.

Jan. 1999

KEN SICARI

In 1956 a handsome boy was born in Brooklyn
In Xaverian H. S. he got an education and some discipline
He earned his B. S. from Wagner's College
Using it to further his insurance knowledge.
He married and then he got a divorce
Because he was the proverbial workhorse.
Still he took some time to play a little game
GAME-oh yes-Kimberly is her name
Besides work and roller-bladeing, he loves to ski
Out in the field - he became a big help to me.
He's noted for being a financial planner
Delivering winning customer service in his inimitable manner.
By locating a lost client who was broke and terminally ill
He undertook a mission of mercy-for the policy was in effect still
By helping "Bill" live in comfort the remainder of his life
See why he was given "real LIFE stories "award with no strife
Ken Sicari - "MetLife and Newsweek" congratulated you
If you need to protect your family's future-you will too.

Congratulations to you Ken
Call him-he'll be there as soon as he can.

Indebted to you
Ruth "Ma" Bell

KATHERINE LEE TENNYSON.

Some one lost a daughter-some one lost a wife
But I lost a friend-a bright part of my life.
I didn't know until November that she was gravely ill
But I kept on hoping that it not be our God's will.
She passed away quietly-leaving us in shock
Everyone will miss her-especially in her block.
She gave love and grace throughout the community
Helped low-income mothers at every opportunity.
She danced for her church-she danced for fun
The Electric Slide, the Macarena-she could not be outdone.
It's hard to say good-bye to some one you love
And harder for Jack-her only true love
He and her mother will never be the same
And neither will I-whenever I hear her name.
We'll all miss her smile, encouraging word and laugh
Kathy Lee Tennyson-JOY-should be your epitaph.
Rest In Peace Kath.

Inspired by Marcia Comrie
12-7-01

Tre

It's nearing October 26, 2001. I'm preparing to break free.
To go out in the world making Nicole and David a family.
Oops I missed Disneyland
So I'll stop here in Greenbelt, Maryland.
Hmm mm. Here's my Dad, David Lee Holt
Time to hit him like a lightning bolt!
There's my Mom, Nicole Antoinette Jackson.
"Mom! Call Sandra and Dosh
Tell them to hurry to meet their new grandson."
I'm here - 19.5 inches long.
Six pounds 13 ounces with a yell that's strong!
They're so proud they named me after Dad
Since I'll be the third they'll call me Tre...not bad.
Now that I'm here there's a smile on every face
I'm glad I chose my parents and Maryland my birthplace!

01-01-2002

THE "McGHEES"

I have a friend Ola who invited me to Alabama
I'd met her children - Leon a trucker - Connie a "Gamma"
I wondered how it would feel in all reality
To go to one's hometown and meet someone's family.

There was Claude - I met him first
A fast-talking man with an insatiable thirst
Then there was Gipp and Mattie B.
She a chatterbox - he talks slow - staying busy as a bee.

Then there's J. W. talks a lot of trash to keep his ego up
Joyce (his wife) a soft-spoken lady just don't get her dander up
Then I met James he took my heart
We talked and he became a very big part
Of the life I had missed since I'd lost my son
I felt if there was anyone - he could be the one.

The only one not here is Claudie May
We all keep expecting her - from day to day
If she comes I'll take a picture - a picture of them all
To give to Ola, to remember the summer 2000-to hang upon her wall.

7-6-00

Seven fourteen

Yesterday was July l4th - some people think of Bastille Day
But that's nothing to celebrate - it's Carole's 56th birthday
What does a Mom say - when she's proud as punch
Where does she take her to - Chick Filá for lunch?
What can I buy her - she has everything
Maybe coerce her husband to get a diamond ring?
If you were to ask her-"What would you like to receive."
If you really know her - than this you will believe.
(her reply) "My children and my friends and my husband too
all of them being here-I'd be happy through and through
it's not the presents that they bring-that doesn't really count
I don't care how much they spend or the real amount
But if they can't be here or forget to call
Next year I'll fix them and won't be home at all." (smile)

7-15-00

BROOK'S CHURCH

Dedicated to Winifred

To you Mom from all your family
From Barbados to England's Piccadilly
They said, if you took us all and left the church
We believe our 10% would leave them in a lurch.
But what we do ? How do we repay a mom like you
That's always in our corner and always been true blue.
Graham — spoiled by you and from each girl
The apple of your eye - your genuine black pearl
When he'd get mad and storm out the door
We watched you drink a cup of tea - and pace the floor.
Then there's us girls Pat, Eglah and Melverdine
We thought we were big enough - then came Julie and Clovine
But today we're here to show you just how dear you are
Not with flowers, candy or a ride in anyone's car
No matter what we give - something made or something bought
It could never be enough to let you know the thought
We carry deep inside from your children, grands, great-grands and more
We want you to know - Mom - we love you not only today
Also the other three sixty-four.

For
Winifred Greaves
5-6-00

"what a pair"

have you ever looked at some one in your life
that are a couple - loving husband and loving wife
they seem so different - just like day and night
them being together - you think they don't look right?

One is quiet and one chatty and loud
What can one say about the other - indicating they are proud
Maybe you can't see it but to them it's clear
Just how much they mean to each other, what they hold so dear.

One maybe vigorous, up and steady going
The other - laid back, silent but all knowing
One loves every one and seems so full of fun
The other in the background - helps to get a job well done.

Till you see them look at each other with a twinkle in their eye
What passes from one to the other - you're my woman you're my guy
From then on your whole perspective maybe will change
You'll see them in a different light by just that one exchange.

1-15-00

dedicated to Rev. and Robert Harrod.

"Welcome"

what would make you want to join a church
is it for the "lord or maybe a spouse - you're on the search
is it for the preacher or the teacher that you seem to heed
is it having a family or someone to talk to that you need?
is it being among Christians to replenish your soul
To listen to some one else tell us things we were never told
To see new faces, how they walk, talk or act
Are these some of the things to bring us on back?
In contrast to all in significance it maybe pale
But to me it rates an 11 on my Richter scale
It's the hospitality that will open any door
Door to a newcomer; stranger, outcast or more.
As a visitor or new resident the welcome is the first to show.
Are you ignored by those who talk to only ones they know?
Or welcomed with a perfunctory handshake - as on their way they go
If you're made to feel at home - affection for that church will grow.
So you see sometimes its that special welcome mat
The one that makes you feel "I am all of that"
With that little hug and a show of love
Helps with your decision - more than all the things above

2-9-00

"THE MAN"

Mental prayer with life and passion
Your body will be filled with love and compassion
Making Him the subject of meditation
Learning His ways - there is no limitation.
He is the light of the world - in, by and for Him be enlighten
Your life will be illuminated and your hopes heighten.
He is the tree of desire under whose shadow we'll refresh
Knowing we are bone of His bone -flesh of His flesh.
He is living Well of Jacob - to wash away all stains
Washing all doubts - whether mental or physical pains.
If you go to Him - observe His words, actions and affection
By means of His brace we learn to speak, act an be His living reflection.

4-10-00

"FAITH"

I often think of the saying "Keep the Faith"-I don't think we should keep it
But let it loose
Through our thoughts, words and actions by doing things for others
You build and put it all to use
Live by faith - in the Son of God and put your fears to rest
Faith of substance, evidence of things not seen will put it to a test.

God has provided ample residence as a basis for faith - when you ask for a sign
Faith is small-blessed are those that have not seen but believes "it's my life-line."
To nourish faith - read your Bible and a scripture reading
With faith-burdens are lightened-nothing is misleading.

Faith is like planting a new garden and seeing the harvest
Knowing you had nothing to do with it-if you're really honest
My favorite Bible verse "You walk by faith-not by sight."
All though you can not see-you still can walk be it day or night.

"ISN'T THAT FAITH."

5 14-00

To Reverend Joe - 2000

Ms. Ward called me to her, said "I'd like a favor."
I thought - what have I done - do I need Rev. Harrod and the Savior?
She smiled and said "It's pastor appreciation time
Can you do us a favor and put something into rhyme?"
I thought about the pastor-nicknamed the one with a plan
I told her I'd try and do the best I can.
I once was requested to take a picture monthly
I'm lucky if I catch him bi or tri-monthly
To get him and his wife together is a chore
I've had to run up the aisle to catch them at the door.
I'm not doing my job-can't get a good shot
He's doing his - some will agree and some will not.
But in this year I think you will agree
There's a lot, about him that puzzles you and me.
He says he's from Arkansas and I heard he loves fish
But where did he get the taste for ackee-that's a Caribbean dish
Barbeque ribs he loves to fix and to eat
Not like Clinton-if he loses this job at least he can cook the meat.
Or open up a restaurant call it Joe's B. B. Q> shack
Let Dr. Dode, Jessie and Jasmine fix the greens with fat-back.
If you see him only in church - you see only one side
At a cook-out if you saw him - you'd know he's qualified
See him on the golf course waiting to give Tiger a play
See him on Jamaica Avenue with his girls shopping for the day.
You'd find he's not only our pastor - but a family man
Like all men he tries wearing three hats whenever Dode says he can
To balance his life with God and his church
Let's have fresh fish - Let's go fish for perch.
The poem is over I've had my say
Go on Rev. Joe and do everything your way:

10-24-00

THE ANSWER

Our children ask questions and requests
Putting our minds and pocketbooks through all tests
Sometimes you can give the help or even an answer
Other times you evade the issue like an agile dancer.
An answering machine picks up your call "Leave a message after the tone."
You feel stupid, talking into silence - will my request be heard on this telephone?
You talk to your next door neighbor - he has an answer for everything
He might not always be right or wrong but he can be real annoying.
With you, your neighbor or the answering machine is there an answer that's
         Always right?
We know of one who knows it all and will answer day or night
Not like the machine - we know our message will be heard
Our answer may take time or come so quick we think it is absurd.
When you get the answer you feel ashamed, humble that you were in doubt
That with prayer, faith and trust He has heard you out
He is the only one that has the answer for everything
He never tires of your asking or the questions that you bring.
He knows when our requests are genuine needs or if He must redirect
He'll forgive all the sins we confess as we genuflect
Remember He's always there and hears our call
And He has the right answer for one and for all.

         3-14-00

ADDING SAUCE TO YOUR SOUL

"ARE YOU TOO OLD?"

I once said, "Sex is something you never forget."
But suppose you're a senior citizen-and hadn't tried it yet
A woman — like a piano - if it's in good condition
Both can be played by a prospective musician.

No matter how long either's been around
Both can be enjoyed with a little turnaround
For the woman - make sure your player - you screen
On the outside you show age - inside you're just a teen.

Age is not a factor - if it's well-cared for
Just make sure - you've checked out- the one who is to score
Like an old violin - the music can be sweet
So if it's the first time or not - it can be a real, real treat.

"NEVER TOO OLD."

11-10-00

EXERCISE

People look at me - some say "You're so fat."
I look in the mirror and know I'm not all of that
Some say menopause makes you gain the weight
But I find it has more to do with who is your mate
The best exercise in the world - I call it sex
That's why a lot of women - find it with an ex
The less you get the more you gain
I know I'm not pretty neither am I vain
But if I had to do it over - I'd be thin as a rail
I'd live on sex and never have to look at the scale
Because then every thing would be every thing
My body, my walk, my whole life would swing
So at my age I'll just keep my friend
The fat and the scale to the bitter end.

6-3-99

"The Male Heart"

I wrote last year-sex was good exercise for a woman
Today I read - hot sweaty sex was good for the man
I also said - good sex would keep our weight down
For the man it's like a game of football or a run through out the town.
They can cut major heart attacks or stroke in half
Having sex four or five times a week-don't make me laugh
How about three times a week at least twenty minutes long
Our men brag and talk about doing it all night long.
To us they do get sweaty and out of breath
But it seems like minutes 'til they fall over like they're dead.
Since mild or moderate levels help their cardiovascular effect
I'll settle for that for his heart and my aftereffect.
Some men suffer fatal cerebral strokes while having sex
Mostly they're unfaithful, having extramarital, a prostitute or an ex
High alcohol or Viagra could also be a factor
Get it anyway lady tell him you're his benefactor
Trying to prolong his life with you
So baby whatever it takes - do what you have to do.

11-30-00

MENTAL BLOCK

Why is it there's so many things that we seem to block out
Is it because we don't want to remember or even think about?
You can remember some things if they're good or bad
You can remember some things if they're happy or even sad.

Yet you can't remember if you had sex with whom or why
If it was last night - did you help or even try
You can't remember what he looked like or remember his face
If you are promiscuous you might not remember his race.

Did I not remember cause I wanted to forget
Cause I didn't want to go home and feel a slight regret
Regret because I didn't want to go home - wishing I could have stayed
Remembering it was a long, long time since I had been really laid.

Now that I'm home here comes the mental block I can't remember the size, color or whose cock
Should I go back and try again - but back to where
The place I don't remember of even being there.
My body feels relief and I'm home all in a sweat
Let the mental block take over and I'll just forget.

6-9-99.

OVERSEXED?

They talk about being oversexed at fifty-one
Some men say, "It's over-my sex life is done."
But ladies remember it's only menopause
    Time to enjoy-time for applause.
Applause because you've finally reached the age
    If you're married or recently became engage.
        Sex is really now-not a hassle but fun
    Now you can really enjoy-sex has just begun
        No more worries of getting pregnant
Or listening or waiting for a crying infant.
    By now kids are grown or moved out
No one bursting in-you can holler or even shout.
    He might say "She is quiet normally
Now she's progressive-doesn't she know we're elderly."
    Am I over-sexed cause I can call the shot
Wanting sex for breakfast, lunch or maybe not?
    Waiting for night-no matter what
Can say "let's go again-I seem to have forgot."
Over-sexed-cause I'm relaxed can look longer up
    I'll even let him look up - I'll get on the top.
If some one says "You're having a raging hormone"
    Enjoy it-your sex-life is now full-blown.
    Once or twice a week or a day
Now it's time to say "Let's do it my way."

DO YOU CARE WHAT THEY SAY?
YOU'RE IN THE DRIVER'S SEAT TODAY
IF YOU'RE THINKING-"HE CAN'T KEEP UP WITH ME."
LOOK OUT FOR YOU-PUT VIAGRA IN HIS TEA.

12-13-01

Once My Dream

I thought the other day - how rich I could be
instead of giving it away I could have charged a fee
I could have got some money just for being bad
Now that I am old - I realize what I had
When I was young I thought that making love was for love
I could have had sex, money, love and all of the above
From the time I was in my twenties this I really know
I'd wanted to be a Madame with my private peep-show
To be a voyeur or even to participate
But now at my age it's much to late to even date
But now with STD or the dreaded AIDS
I'd have been an executioner-as they worked their trades
So I guess that I'm lucky - I called it love-it was free
Got me working for the whites-scrubbing on a knee
I could have been a rich, convicted Madame of a brothel
Or a rich, convicted Madame lolling in a jail cell
But I'm only a poor black woman - who only had a dream
Living with only black coffee-no sugar or no cream
So think of all the men and women who never met me
They're alive and healthy and my conscience is still free,

2-i8-OI

"SHACKING"

what I'm about to say - church people won't agree

would you buy a pig - one that is unseen?

To me a marriage certificate is just a piece of paper

It doesn't come with a guarantee to keep him from a caper

It doesn't serve to fence in spouses who are prone to stray

Doesn't give you permission to test if he's straight or gay

If he cheated when you went together - he'll go from a cheating boyfriend
    To a cheating husband

At least if you had lived together you'd know that in a second.

When you're dating you only see him on his good behavior & he's
    smelling clean

But if you shack awhile you'll know how he acts when he's hungry & gets mean

Does he shower, use deodorant, toothpaste & pick-up after himself

Or leave his dirty socks & drawers on the floor & his bridgework on the shelf

You only see the best of him when you two go out

He'll spend his last dime on you, you see without a doubt

But sometimes after you've been together for a little while

You might change your mind - about walking down that aisle.

6-20-99

TELL ME

Men will confess - "I've been cheating and I don't know why"
The why is not the question it's the fact he told a lie
I was told a stiff dick has no conscience when I was very young
Before I'd even thought of having sex by dick or by tongue.

Men say "I was drunk" or "she came on to me."
I never even thought of it - till she got down on her knee
For sex, to beg or just to plea
To me it was a piece that's free."

Now that he's confessed what am I supposed to do
To forgive him as he says "I'm sorry - I love only you."
Or remember once you cheat you always cheat
And kick him to the curb for his lies and his deceit.

3-15-99

Woman's day at the "VAULT."

I went to a reading - boy did I have fun
Everyone talked of sex and things they had done
I thought of things past and wiggled in my seat
The words were cool and sensual but filled the room with heat

Sex is something like riding a bike - you don't forget
I don't think about it often but I don't have to fret
I use vaseline when sex becomes an issue
When it's all over - wipe my fingers with a tissue.

But if I ever decide I'd like a man - I want one that's young
Not like another old one with an active tongue
I'd teach him how to satisfy - he'd be the best in town
I'd teach him what to do - if it's up or down.

But right now I'll depend upon my finger
Think about the melodies that always seem to linger
I don't have to worry about AIDS or S. T. D.
I only have to worry about satisfying little old me.

Sex is the thing that keeps you young and your skin tight
It keeps you always smiling and your eyes real bright
You don't have as many headaches and less pain
And it seems much better when you hear the rain.

So ladies remember no matter how old you get
Sex is something you don't ever really forget
That you can look up longer than he can look down
So girl remove that frown and your nightgown.

GET BUSY AND ENJOY.

3-21-99
1

9 - 11 /

W T C